Not Your Mother's Book...

On Being a Woman

Created by
Dahlynn McKowen
and **Ken McKowen**

Published by
Publishing Syndicate

 PO Box 607
Orangevale California 95662
www.PublishingSyndicate.com

Not Your Mother's Book...
On Being a Woman

*We would like to thank the many individuals
who granted us permission to reprint their stories.
See the complete listing beginning on page 292.*

Created and edited by Dahlynn McKowen and Ken McKowen

Cover and book design by Publishing Syndicate
Cover photo: Solovyova Lyudmyia/Shutterstock.com
Copyeditor: Terri Elders

Published by
Publishing Syndicate
PO Box 607
Orangevale California 95662

www.PublishingSyndicate.com
www.Facebook.com/PublishingSyndicate
Twitter: @PublishingSynd

Print Edition ISBN: 978-1-938778-00-1
EPUB Digital Edition ISBN: 978-1-938778-01-8
Library of Congress Control Number 2012916846

Printed in Canada

This book is a collaborative effort. Writers from all over the world submitted their work for consideration, with 64 stories making the final cut. All contributors are compensated for their stories and are invited to take part in a media campaign.

Publishing Syndicate strongly encourages you to submit your story to one of its many anthologies. You'll find information on how to do so at the end of this book, starting on page 294.

~~ To my mother, Scharre Johnson ~~

The release of this first book in the
Not Your Mother's Book series falls on
my mother's 69th birthday, which is apropos
because she is daring, sexy and a bit kinky!

A two-time cancer survivor, I never thought
my mom would make it to her 69th birthday,
but she did.
And with enough wine,
she'll be with us another 69 years!

In all seriousness, my mother
is my hero and my best friend.
This book *is* my mother's book.
Happy birthday, Mom.

~~ Dahlynn

Content

Acknowledgments   x
Introduction   xii

1 Keeping Up Appearances   1
Worse Than Zombie Warts   T'Mara Goodsell   2
W—The *Other* Scarlet Letter   Terri Spilman   6
Dinner Dance Drama   Pam Suwinsky   9
Granny Pants   Elizabeth Bussey Sowdal   14
The Must-Have   Wendy Nelson   17
Suck It Up   Linda O'Connell   20
Sarong, So Right   Debra Ayers Brown   24
Dressing to Kill is Killing Me Terri Duncan   28

2 Worth Our Weight in Gold   35
Honey, You're a Fat Ass   Terri Spilman   36
The Revolving Door   Elynne Chaplik-Aleskow   40
Size 14 is Not a Curse   Mary Horner   43
Got Love Handles?   Donna Collins Tinsley   47
Zigzagging   Caroleah Johnson   51
It's Gotta Be the Hair   Mary-Lane Kamberg   54
High Five   Alice Muschany   57
Starve Yourself Thin   Marijo Herndon   60

3 They're Called Boobs!   65
Tan Lines   Susan Nickerson   66
Booby Trapped   Erika Hoffman   70
Everything's Bigger in Texas   Kendra Alvey   75
Up Front   Terri Elders   85

Battle-Dressed Breasts   Laurel McHargue   89
Almost Barely Complete   Valerie Benko   93
Cream or Sugar?   Dianna Graveman   97
The Ice Bra Cometh   Monica Giglio   101

4 Hear Me Roar   107
Harley and the Harridan   Janet Hall Svisdahl   108
For Better or For Worse   Ginger Kenchel   114
No Mountain Too High   Kathe Campbell   117
Backing Up   Caroleah Johnson   120
Life's a Classroom   Elsilee Patterson   124
The Pinup Girl   Joyce Newman Scott   128
Smackdown   Barbara Carpenter   132
Stirred, Not Shaken   Mary Eileen Williams   136

5 Just Saying   141
Not-So-Sweet Revenge   Marcia Byalick   142
Vajazzle My What?   Terri Spilman   146
The Princess and the Pimp   Ellen Denton   149
Peace in Pandemonium   Marijo Herndon   153
Blind-Sighted   Pat Nelson   157
Tawdry Behavior   Laura Farkas   162
It All Depends   Nancy Withers   165
Will He Notice Me Then?   Sandie Lee   168

6 Stand Up!   171
Your Hard Drive's Corrupted   Sylvia Bright-Green   172
Three and I'm Out   Kathleene Baker   177
For Your Convenience   Tina Traster   180
Give a Woman a Gun   Sallie Rodman   184
The Price is Right   Ruth Littner   187
The Force of Eds   Sallie Wagner Brown   191

| Come Rain or Shine | Cathi LaMarche | 198 |
| Spam-in-a-Can | Sandie Lee | 202 |

7 Never Again!

		207
It's a Wrap	Cappy Hall Rearick	208
Sitting Room Only	Janet Sheppard Kelleher	214
Only a Coincidence	Georgia A. Hubley	218
To the Brink and Back	Sioux Roslawski	223
And Me Without a Crotch	Rose Ella Putnam	226
No More Should	Lisa McManus Lange	229
The Windy Dress	Glady Martin	233
Hair Gone Wild	Stacey Gustafson	236

8 Sense and Sensibility

		239
Egged On	Terri Elders	240
Die-Hard Eager Beaver	Mary A. Berger	246
Single and Searching	Sara Foore	249
Dance Hall Girl	Ellen Denton	253
Mystified by Women	Gregory Lamping	261
Age is Just a Number	Karen Gaebelein	268
A Chocolate Coffee Paradox	Diana M. Amadeo	272
A Catholic Schoolgirl's Primer	Carole Ann Moleti	276

NYMB Creators	282
Contributor Bios	284
Story Permissions	292
Photo Credits	293
Publishing Syndicate	294
More NYMB Titles	295

Acknowledgments

Creating a completely new book series is quite the undertaking, and with this book being the first in the *Not Your Mother's Book* (NYMB) series, we graciously accepted as much help as we could get!

Thank you, Terri Elders, for being our copyeditor extraordinaire. The images of you with a red pen in one hand and whip in the other makes us smile.

Thank you, Michele Cemo, for reading tons of story submissions and offering your recommendations. Have you stopped laughing yet?

Thank you, Steve Elders, for your expert advice as we created our style guide for the NYMB series; your guidance will keep our NYMB books fresh, hip and modern. Your mother raised you well.

Thank you, Kathy Baker, for being our look-see lady, catching all those little things we missed in the manuscript before it went to print. You (affectionately) suck, big time!

Thank you, Alysha Hinson, for your wonderful idea regarding changing the title of one of the stories in the book. You know which one, as do we, but we'll let everyone else figure it out!

Thank you, Gregory Lamping, for being the only male brave enough to have a story in a book on being a woman.

Thank you, Paul Krupin, for overseeing our media and public relations campaign. Through your company Direct Contact PR (www.DirectContactPR.com), you have never let us down, helping us navigate the world of promotion and making our books shine!

Thank you, NYMB co-creators, for joining us on this amazing journey. We appreciate you jumping into this project with us and look forward to your books' releases!

Thank you, Shawn, for once again putting up with Mom and Dad's craziness in creating yet another book!

And most of all, thank you to those who have graciously shared their stories with us. We couldn't have done it without you.

~~ Dahlynn and Ken McKowen

Introduction

I was in a queer mood,
thinking myself very old:
but now I am a woman again—
as I always am when I write.

~~Virginia Woolf

As a woman and a writer, I've always loved this saying.

English novelist Adeline Virginia Woolf (1882-1941) was a woman before her time. Her writings were almost too modern for her readers, but she stayed true to her words. For this reason, her writings and poems made her one of the foremost literary giants of the 20th century.

While Woolf has her critics, her writing was highly experimental, and she brilliantly adopted a nonfiction narrative style, drawing on personal experience. She was an innovator when it came to the written word, especially her poems. And her work was, at times, risqué, which, to the prudish and upper-crust English, was scandalous. But I bet that those same naysayers secretly read her work behind closed doors!

In this new century, sexual ambivalence has taken a backseat to an emerging sexual revolution when it comes to writing. And when I say "sexual," I'm not talking obscene or pornographic material. Woman today are truly alive and comfortable in their own skins. They are successful, beautiful, giving, inspiring and exude

womanhood more than any generation before them. They have come
into their own with all barrels loaded, cocked and ready to go. There
is no stopping them.

That's what you'll find when you read this book; within
these pages are stories from female writers who aren't afraid to
share what is on their minds and in their souls. Their stories are
hip, edgy, raw, funny and a bit raunchy. They have much to say
and now they have a platform to say it.

Virginia would be proud.

~~ Dahlynn McKowen

NYMB . . . On Being a Woman

CHAPTER ONE

Keeping Up Appearances

The things we do to look great . . .

Worse Than Zombie Warts

by

T'Mara Goodsell

It was supposed to be my little secret. I was going to slip into a pair when I got out of the shower. I'd hang around the house in them when I wasn't expecting company. I'd wear them outside, but only to run to my mailbox. Or I'd wear them on a really cold day under a coat. No one would have to know.

I'm not a robe- or sweatpants-kind of person. Robes are too bulky and sweatpants are too much of a lie. They wouldn't fool anyone. The only sweating that would take place in them would be when I had to lean way over to scrape smashed brownie crumbs off the sofa with my nail—spatula-style— while watching television.

I had planned on ordering them online, but . . . shhhh . . . I didn't want my computer to know. The reason is because when my middle-schooler got that ugly wart partially under his toe-nail, I Googled "warts" and for months afterwards, my computer unexpectedly punished me with pop-up photos of warts. Big warts. Little warts. Warts in varying degrees of wartiness. It was like reading one of those forwarded online jokes where you're supposed to see if you can spot the little dot in the picture and then a really ugly zombie suddenly jumps out to scare you.

I did do a noncommittal Google search, but I cleverly sandwiched it between legitimate research on whether Bill Nighy, the British actor, is the same person as Bill Nye the Science Guy (not) and whether Beethoven really was as cute as he looks in his statue (possibly). You know—to throw the computer off track. The search did show I could buy what I wanted at a nearby store without my computer finding out and shaming me.

So I went to the store late on a Saturday night, when no one else shops except a few other crowd-hating women like me. Problem was, this was a bath store, and I had no idea where they would stock my item. I tried to look unapproachable, but I have this horrible affliction where I am the most approachable person in the world. Plus, the employees were evidently looking for an excuse to get out of stocking duties. One came to help me, an adorable young man of about 20.

Right away I had to decide: 1) Did I want to admit what I wanted to him? Or 2) Wander by aimlessly and pretend I didn't need his help? Since I am not the quickest of thinkers, I decided on a compromise: 3) Mumble.

"Can you tell me where I can find *pphhmmmaa jhhmmmms*?"

"Excuse me?" he politely responded.

"You know—*pphhmmmaa jhhmmmms*."

He looked at me, thoroughly perplexed. I knew I could

only let him say "excuse me" so many times. Thus, I finally took a deep breath and admitted what I so longed to have caress my body. That was when the walkie-talkie appeared in his hands. It was too late. Of course, the walkie-talkie was connected to the store's P.A. system. It moved to his mouth as if in slow motion, then he uttered to the entire store, "Jay, where do we have the PAJAMA JEANS?"

So there it was, literally broadcast in public, that I wanted sweats that impersonated jeans. Jeans that flunked out of Jeans School for complete failure to work. Clothing lower on the clothing chain than jeans. Defective-gened non-jeans. An article of clothing born from jeans' less classy side of the family.

Jay was up on a ladder, which made him both loud *and* visible. "PAJAMA JEANS!?!" he shouted. Then he had to think out loud a bit, and into the speaker: "PAJAMA JEANS . . . PAJAMA JEANS . . . hmmm . . . wait! There's a whole display of PAJAMA JEANS in the middle of the aisle."

With that, my young clerk paraded me up and down the aisles, and I drifted after him like the Lazy Ass Jeans float in the Macy's Thanksgiving Day Parade. But he couldn't find the display. We passed pretty much every customer in the store, and it turned out due to the sale there were quite a few more than usual. Another all-store broadcast ensued, drawing yet more clerks and even helpful customers. Now everyone in the store knew I was buying jean imposters. A crowd began to gather around the pajama jean display—seemingly every one of those dear, helpful people wanted to make sure my derriere was covered in ample amounts of pretend denim. Sweatless sweatpants—riveted with pocket studs—for the serious lounger.

"They're not for me," I said lamely when we finally approached the crowd. "They're for . . ." Only I couldn't think of who they'd be for. Not only am I the world's worst liar, embarrassment made any blood left in my brain rush straight to my face. I gave it up and hung my head. "OK, but I probably won't wear them in public. Much."

One woman, bless her heart, decided to step up and rescue me from the humiliation. "I have them, too," she whispered.

Hooray for human kindness. And hooray for these fleecy mullets of jeandom. I am a hardcore lounger with a soft-core rear end to prove it. Just call before you come over so I can change.

T'Mara lounging in her Pajama Jeans!

W—The *Other* Scarlet Letter

by
Terri Spilman

*Ah, but let her cover the mark as she will, the pang
of it will be always in her heart—and on her ass.*

The above was adapted—by me—from Nathaniel Hawthorne's classic novel, *The Scarlet Letter*. Let me explain why.

Fat-bottomed girls may make the rockin' world go round, but they sure have a hell of a time finding an attractive pair of jeans that fit. Muffin Top. Camel Toe. Lumpy Ass. Too Long. High Water. Can't Breathe. Thunder Thighs. No, that's not a modern-day version of the seven dwarfs. They are the seven phases of trying on jeans.

Shopping for jeans has earned a place on my dreaded-things-to-do list, along with trying on bathing suits. And the skinny jean trend is only adding to my frustration. As a fat-bottomed girl, I have limited options if I want to wear skinny jeans. I can either shove my muffin top into my bra and change my name to Linda Vaughn—the first lady of racing who has the most recognizable set of giant tatas in the motorsports world—or shop in the only department with a letter more controversial than the "A" on Hester Prynne's chest—the *Women's* Department. Yes, the always-hushed department for bigger ladies found deep in the bowels of major department stores, usually in a corner next to the restroom. For some reason, there is a stigma attached to shopping in the Women's section. It's actually an under-used resource. Instead of going up in size, the "W" simply allows for more expansion space where you need it.

The Women's Department is always poorly marked. For example, unknown to me, Macy's recently did a total department reset. I almost walked out of the store with a pair of husky-sized Wrangler jeans with an Angry Bird on the ass before I figured out I was in the Tween Boy department.

To add to the confusion, Macy's has even changed the name of the "Misses" department to "Ladies." Let me tell you, I still consider myself a lady even though I may need a little more material on occasion to cover my polite behind. Like now, after a holiday cheese-ball binge.

Designers also need to get on the bandwagon for us "Women." No one wants to be chubby. Most of us put a lot of thought and effort in trying not to be. In the meantime, we still need and want something cute to wear that doesn't have elastic around the waist or resembles a smock. I'm secretly hoping a young Hollywood starlet won't be able to lose her baby weight, and thus become the new voice and designer extraordinaire for "W" clothes.

I heard a piece of weight loss advice while randomly switching radio stations on the way home from the mall: "Instead of using chocolate to ease your stress, just think of Jesus. I know it sounds cheesy, but it works for me." Cheese? Did someone say cheese? After hearing the advice, all I could think about was a "Cheesus"—a Cheeto that looks like Jesus. The divine willpower that person must have had. Who could refuse an extra crunchy Cheesus?

My skinny-jean curiosity peaked after a girls' night out. I was the only mom rocking a pair of Kohl's "W" jeans. The rest of the group was wrapped in Lucky Brand denim. I swear they were walking in slow motion, with their Sweet N Low-covered asses swinging in synchronicity. So off to Lucky Brands I went to buy me some Sweet N Low skinny jeans. But sweet Cheesus! I couldn't even cram one of my legs into a pair. Then I went to the grocery store and bought the other kind of Sweet'N Low.

Now for my own quote, hopefully to live in eternity like Hawthorne's work:

> *I am woman,*
> *hear me roar,*
> *as I squeeze into skinny jeans no more,*
> *—thanks to the "W."*

Dinner Dance Drama

by

Pam Suwinsky

In February 2009, I went to a semiformal fundraising dinner dance sponsored by St. Francis of Assisi Parish in Sacramento. In planning what to wear, I wasn't sure I remembered all the necessary items, as I hadn't been that dressed up since New Year's Eve 2004.

Fortunately, a month prior, I'd already decided on a dress to wear—a sequined A-line cocktail dress that belonged to my mother-in-law. I carefully chose my accessories: sparkly black heels, a tiny, vintage beaded purse, a fringed wrap, crystal chandelier earrings and an ever-so-dainty wristwatch. Then I spent three weeks talking with my girlfriends about what kind of underwear to wear with a cocktail dress. The dress wasn't at all clingy, but it was drapey and flowy, so any lumps and bumps would be my enemies for that evening. The possibilities and suggestions seemed endless: full slip or half-slip, chemise slip or body shaper, stockings or pantyhose, bra built into the slip or separate, no-show panties or the kind that are part of panty-hose? I had to decide.

The big day had arrived, and I'd finally settled on my undergarment selections: a full-length chemise slip, a package of thigh-high stockings with lace elastic tops, and a pair of no-show panties I had found in one of my dresser drawers, with the tags still on. The panties had a wide band of lace around the waist and also around both legs.

I'm sure I've nailed this look, I said to myself, pleased over my selection. I began to get dressed; I put on the panties, bra, slip and the stockings straight out of the package. But there was a run in one leg of the stockings. I reached into the same drawer where I had found the panties and came across a pair of sheer black pantyhose—which had only been worn one time before. I donned the hose and decided they looked great and worked well with the rest of my ensemble. *Perfect!*

I then stepped into my sparkly heels and my ankles buckled—I toppled right out of them! Thoughts of Lucy Ricardo flitted through my mind. I put on the shoes once more and marched around my house to get used to walking in heels again. I walked on carpet, linoleum, hardwood and cement until I felt confident I'd be able to make it into the Dante Club and across the floor without falling sideways out of my shoes.

At the dance, a friend on the parish council invited me to sit at the table with the council and the parish priest. My first dance—a jitterbug with a member of the parish council—was fun, but mid-spin, I started feeling something pulling around my hips. *Oh, oh. What's that?* About halfway through the dance, my partner needed to stop, patting his chest and apologizing for his pacemaker. I thanked him and then made a beeline for the ladies' room. Once inside, I found that my pantyhose were sliding and twisting down my hips! I took them completely off and started again, making sure the feet were on properly and that there were no twists in the legs. The crotch was in place, the hip seams were aligned, and the waistband was on target. *OK, that should work.*

The next dance was a line dance. I didn't like it much. I found that as soon as I learned the steps, I got bored and then got annoyed when people bumped into me. Suddenly, there was a tug around my lower hip. *Not AGAIN!*

Once in the safety of a bathroom stall, I found the culprit; it was the no-show panties. The elastic around the waist had started to curl down and the panties were sliding down my hips, taking the pantyhose with them. I took the panties off, put them in my tiny purse, ran out to the car and put them in the glove compartment.

Next came mingling time. As I moved around the room to chat with old and new friends, I was aware that gaps and wrinkles were forming in my stockings. *Ugh! Ladies' room again.* The culprit this time was the elastic waistband of the pantyhose, which had stretched out so much that they were now 4 inches too big for my waist!

What is going on? Are my undergarments declaring battle with me as they try to escape from under my dress? And now I was facing a major decision: *What am I going to do with my stretched pantyhose?* I thought about taking them off, but I wasn't comfortable wearing neither panties nor pantyhose at a church dance. Plus, it would feel uneven to wear a bra and no panties. Far worse was that bare legs would ruin the look—way too informal for sequins and sparkles. And besides, it was February and my legs were fish-belly white. *No, I'll keep the hose on and keep adjusting them.*

After the dancing and mingling, all attendees were treated to a lovely sit-down dinner and bottles of wine. After dinner, I rested my hand against my throat and found something poking out of the neckline of my dress. *It's just the lining of my dress,* I thought as I pushed it inside the neckline. It came back out. I tried to be discreet as I examined with my fingers what this was, and a sense of horror came over me: *It's my slip!*

Once again in the ladies' room, I saw in the mirror that the A-line of my dress was now looking rectangular. I checked under the dress and found that my full-length slip had worked its way up to my armpits and was making its way out the neck of my dress! *This is war!* I smoothed it out and down, tucked the slip in around the base of my bra to hold it in place, and headed out to join the rest of the partygoers.

It wasn't long before I started to feel a binding around my body. *What now? The dress is straight. The seams are in the right places.* In the ladies' room, I found that my slip had completely twisted around my body so that the right armhole was now in the center of my chest and the left armhole was across my back! And the hem was completely turned around from front to back and again up under my armpits. *Do my undergarments have a mind of their own?*

While I was trying to get everything adjusted, the safety chain of my delicate watch got caught in the lace at the hem of my slip. I was turning and bending and struggling to release it without tearing the fabric when another woman came into the ladies' room and rescued me. Thankfully, she knelt down on the floor and was able to untangle the chain from my slip.

As we stood next to each other in front of the mirror, now brushing our hair and refreshing our lipstick, my helper kept pulling at the scoop neck of her dress. She explained, "My bra won't stay inside my dress!"

Conspiracy theorists, we need to talk . . . .

Granny Pants

by
Elizabeth Bussey Sowdal

I swore that it would never happen to me, but it has. I have become the nightmare of my teenage years. I have grayed and wizened. Bits of me that were once taut are now wiggly and jiggly, and bits of me that used to be loose have frozen up. This I have borne with relative good grace. But today I became my own bête noire.

I bought a pair of Granny Pants. I ought to have bought myself one of those "Queen of Denial" T-shirts too, because I was definitely doing some fast self-talk. After a long day of trying on pair after pair of jeans at store after store, I was ready to give up. I tried on jeans that snapped just below where my bosom currently resides. I tried on jeans that snapped way, way, way lower than that. I tried on jeans that were belled and boot-cut and tapered. I tried on jeans that were "relaxed" and jeans I suspected of being on the verge of a nervous breakdown. I tried on jeans that were the deep, new indigo I'd rejected as a girl for looking dorky, and jeans that looked like they had been worn for a few weeks by an auto mechanic. I think I tried on every pair of jeans in the greater metropolitan area.

And then I found them. The only reason I even tried them on was because they were on sale. I'm a sucker for something on sale. But I loved them! They were almost as comfortable as pajama pants. I preened in front of the mirror. *These look like something Katharine Hepburn would wear,* I thought. *So neat looking, so flattering and so comfortable. Are they a little short though? Nah! I see people wearing their britches all different lengths. They're fine. And sooooo comfortable!*

Why were they so comfortable? I am going to tell you something now that I never, ever thought I would say in a million, billion years—they had a half-elastic waist. And long, loose legs. And square sailor-style pockets. And I loved them. And they weren't Katharine Hepburn pants. They weren't sailor pants. They were Granny Pants, pure and simple.

I have worn all kinds of jeans. For example, I once had elephant-bell hip-huggers that were more patchwork than pant, but were they ever so cool! I had cut the seam out of my jeans and put in a big triangle of brightly-colored material. I was going to wear them to my seventh-grade Sadie Hawkins dance that night. I couldn't sew, and my mom wasn't going to be home in time, so I tried some good old Elmer's glue instead. That didn't work so well, so I stapled them and called it good. I went over to my friend Jane's house. "Wow, Liz! Look at your jeans!" she said, with some worry in her voice. What I heard instead was, "Your jeans are so cool."

"Mom," Jane said, still concerned, "look at Liz's jeans."

"I bet you did those all by yourself, didn't you?" her mother asked me, upon closer inspection of my pants.

"Yes, ma'am, I did," I said, not too modestly.

"Would you like me to just give them a quick going over so your staples don't show so much?" her mother offered. Since one of the staples was, at that very moment, jabbing itself painfully into my calf, I agreed to her kind offer.

In high school, I wore my jeans way, way, way too long so that the cuff would get appropriately frayed and dirty. In the 1980s, I wore super tight jeans in every color of the rainbow. The tighter and brighter, the better they would go with my enormous shoulder pads and gigantic hair.

Then I experienced a decade or so when I could not find any jeans that both fit and looked right. Until yesterday. I wore those jeans today. I asked my daughter if she thought they were too short. "Don't worry, Mom. Nobody will notice." *Uh-oh.* I started to fret and tried to see my reflection in a glass door. And then her words sank in and I had an epiphany: *Nobody will notice. Nobody. Will notice.*

I am now free! Liberated! Released from the dictates of fashion through the sheer perseverance I have shown in surviving this long! I can wear any damn thing I want to wear and nobody will notice!

Goodbye panty hose, hello knee socks! Fair-thee-well heels and howdy-doo driving mocs! Hasta la vista cuffs and collars and waistbands and hello to the wonderful world of jersey knits! Katharine Hepburn, my hind leg! Hellooooo Granny Pants!

The Must-Have

by
Wendy Nelson

I was 14 when they literally walked into my life. Living in a small Canadian town, our only option for shopping was the Sears catalog. At the time, my main mission was to get to that catalog before my two older sisters, so I could pick out what was to be—in my wise estimation—the coolest thing in the entire world, and get it ordered—FAST!

In my quest, I beat my sisters home from swimming lessons that hot July afternoon. Immediately noticing that the flag on the mailbox was down, I ripped open the metal door—ignoring how it burned my hand—and grabbed everything inside. Rushing into the garage, I went to my hiding spot under my father's workbench.

The boots were on page 42, in all their shiny, leather glory. They were slightly above the ankle, all black with inside zippers, and had 3-inch chunky heels. And the toes were rounded—no pointy witch boots for me!

They were perfect. *I had to have them!* I whispered to myself. The only problem was the price. I had some money saved from Christmas and my birthday, but it wasn't enough. I needed time to save more. Using my father's X-Acto knife, I carefully removed the page the boots were on, hoping my sisters wouldn't realize what I'd done.

I worked extra hard that summer of 1989. I picked dandelions until my fingers turned green. I babysat the two little girls next door, even though I was sure they were the spawn of the devil. And through a garage sale, I even sold my favorite stuffed animal—a huge cheetah I had won at Canada's Wonderland amusement park near Toronto. But in my mind, it was all worth it. My mission was clear: get the boots before school started.

All my hard work over the summer paid off and I was successful in reaching my goal, with a few days to spare. It was sweltering the day my mom and I drove into town. We didn't have air conditioning in our big, brown van, but we endured the drive, all in the name of fashion.

My heart thumped like mad during the entire drive; I was going to be the coolest ninth grader—ever! I worried, though: *What if they didn't fit? What if they didn't look the same in real life as opposed to the picture in the catalog? What if some other girl had the same pair?* But knowing they would be perfect, I shoved those thoughts aside.

They weren't perfect. My first day wearing them to school was a mess. But only I knew it. Yes, I received compliments galore. And yes, I was the envy of a lot of girls. But my dream boots were trying to kill me! They pinched and rubbed my skin raw. I struggled with them throughout the day and when I got home, all I wanted to do was scream and throw the boots away.

But I couldn't bring myself to do it. I'd worked hard for those boots and, by God, I wasn't going to let them win. I didn't care that they made a sound when I walked, due to something imbedded in the heel. And I didn't care I had to wear 13 Band-Aids just to keep the blisters at bay. *These boots will not rule me! I will wear them down and be victorious!*

It took me eight months to break them in. The once-stiff leather finally softened and the boots no longer rubbed or pinched. I had won! But my victory was short lived. It was as though my feet grew two sizes overnight and I could no longer squeeze my feet into the boots. *All those months of pain and struggle for only a few days of comfort,* I thought to myself, sadly.

I could have wallowed in the injustice of it all, but I didn't. It's been over 20 years and I still have those boots. They are my reminder that not everything, or everyone, comes perfect. But with a determined spirit, those fleeting moments of sheer pleasure are very much worth a little pain.

Wendy and her famous shoes!

Suck It Up

by
Linda O'Connell

After observing the women in my family who all gab at one time, I learned early to follow two essential survival rules, neither of which is easy to abide by: suck it in and suck it up.

For generations the gutsy women in my family have been constricting their guts. Their opinions however, have never been restricted; retracted sometimes, but we have never held back our thoughts. We are women of our words, and every new husband or boyfriend understands that our mouths are over-stuffed.

We are less concerned with our mouths than our abdomens, though. Grandma's generation wore corsets that had to be laced. Mom's generation wore girdles that made them groan. My undergarments are infused with spandex, and now, my adult granddaughter has discovered body shapers. I bought one, but no matter how I tried to wriggle into that thing, I was unable to squeeze all of me in. I gave up. So what if my belly jiggles a little when I wiggle? I've delivered children, made my contribution. This is the result. I am much more accepting of my flaws than my ancestors were.

I have been a preschool teacher for three decades. Little kids let it all hang out; they have no filter, no fashion sense and I don't have to dress to impress. The only time I'm really concerned about my midsection is when my students perform for their parents and I must address the crowd. I know that most parents are gazing at their darlings, but I still have a lingering fear that all eyes will eventually focus on my pooch. I dreaded having to stand in front of a roomful of young moms. I just knew they were giving me the once over. I once had a body to die for, too.

Over the years, I have learned to expect the unexpected at school performances. Inevitably someone cries, shows off or takes off. This year, my antics were more memorable than those of my students. The class had rehearsed songs and finger plays for the highly anticipated end-of-year moms' tea party. They drew pictures of their mothers and told candid stories about them. The mothers all needed tissues to wipe away tears from laughing so hard and a few actually cried.

My chosen attire for this particular performance was a black skirt—instead of my standard slacks—a silky blouse, and heels, in lieu of my normal flats. But my pooch stuck out when I put on the skirt. I knew I couldn't naturally suck in my gut for any length of time, and my control top panty hose have about as much control over my tummy as the moms did over their kids and their secret-telling. So I scrunched my gut into an old-fashioned crotchless girdle—a spandex belly band with a dozen strategically-positioned foot-long stays that allowed me to giggle without the jiggle. I know these days that Spanx are the in-thing, but I figured I could endure the combined misery of girdle, undies and pantyhose for an hour. "Breathe," I had to remind myself, as I was sure the constriction was depriving my brain of oxygen.

At the presentation, the 15 mothers in attendance were seated in a semicircle in the middle of my classroom. Their children sang songs and performed, and afterwards, served their mothers refreshments. Then they snuggled in their mothers' laps while I read a story, which made the kids giggle and the mothers nod knowingly.

After the story, I was in the midst of passing out flyers and was half way around the semi-circle when I dropped my papers and bent to retrieve them. That's when I felt the constriction in my midsection rise to my throat as my girdle made its great escape! It rolled south and my flab escaped north, just like a muffin top. My face went flush and my heart beat rapidly, for I was sure all eyes were on me. I quickly excused myself and waddled to the tiny-tots' bathroom at the far end of my classroom where I removed the damned thing. Finally, I breathed a sigh of relief. I was so happy to be free and to be me. I pencil-rolled the girdle, folded it in half and I shoved it under my blouse. I then walked over to my desk chair and discreetly shoved it down into my purse.

I finished passing out the papers, said a few inspirational parting words and thanked all of the moms for coming. As the last of the group headed out the door, I kicked off my high heels and slipped my weary feet into my flats. I then bent over to retrieve my heels to toss into my oversized purse when I realized a mother and child had returned; they were now standing directly in front of me. At that exact moment, while opening my purse to add my heels, my white girdle unfurled and popped out like a Jack-in-the-box!

Speechless, the mom looked down at my purse, and then she looked at me. I looked down at my purse and then at her. We stared wide-eyed at one another for a few moments.

"Well, let me give you a hug. I want to thank you for everything," she said appreciatively.

Believe me, when I hugged her, I wanted to thank her for not mentioning what she'd just witnessed. Normally I would blow this sort of thing off, but this woman was a high-profile reporter on a local TV station; I was so afraid to turn on the morning news and hear her editorial commentary about a teacher with an escaping girdle!

Usually it's the kids who act up, cause a ruckus or even a great escape. This year, it was the teacher who was unable to suck it in. I just had to suck it up.

Sarong, So Right

by

Debra Ayers Brown

Fresh-mowed grass, chirping birds, and my worst nightmare signaled summer.

Yep, you guessed it—swimsuit season.

In my tweens, teens and twenties, I pranced, preened and always pinched less than an inch. It felt so good. It felt so right. I thought I'd love wearing a swimsuit forever. But now, I looked in the mirror, thinking pot pies, too much Thai—and thunder thighs.

Ugh.

I would avoid swimsuits if not for my young-adult daughter, Meredith. Living on the coast, I'd been forced to swim, go boating or frolic on the beach since her birth. How could I miss the family fun?

Truth is, I loved the coast. Each May, I'd drag out my old swimsuits for Meredith's critical inspection, only to receive a failing grade. I would then find myself at the department store and in front of a three-way funhouse mirror, clad in the latest swimsuit fashion. My frame of mind that day dictated whether the mirror showed an image bigger than life or not.

So while browsing the swimsuit aisles one day with my daughter, I looked for garments to disguise those pot pies, too much Thai food and thunder thighs. I wanted to find one I could love forever. The vast assortment featured conservative one-piece swimsuits, sleek two-pieces and itsy-bitsy suits favored by the young and those obese "Big Mama" women in booty shorts.

With the "Big Mama" image in mind, I scanned the sizes: petite, regular, tall, plus and long torso. I focused on my body issues and searched for the perfect swimsuit. I longed for a miracle-suit-turned-shapeware suit to transform my 5-foot-3-inch body into a slender, 6-foot-tall Victoria's Secret model, complete with long legs and endless airbrushing.

Where are the smoke and mirrors when I need them? I thought. Reality tended to suck.

"With all these suits," I said to Meredith, "there must be one that will fit." I perused the racks. "I never know which size will work." I studied the flowered, striped and solid fabrics. "I wish designers would realize normal women need to look good in swimsuits, too."

I pondered the swimsuit dilemma for adult women over 30. We deserved a swimsuit to make us feel good even if we weren't a size 0 or below. Wasn't sub-0 reserved for our freezers anyway? Even women built like brick houses should be able to find a garment with the mortar in all the right places.

"Magazines tout ways to camouflage hips, tummies and big boobs. But I've never been able to pull it off," I confided in my daughter. "I wish swimsuits really disguised the flaws."

"They do," Meredith said. "Look at the labels."

"But if it sucks you in somewhere," I said, already gasping for breath, preparing for the inevitable, "then you poke out somewhere else."

Regardless, I grabbed as many swimsuits in petite, regular, tall and long torso as I could and carried them to the musty dressing room with a wish for a good fit, high heels to try them on in, and, of course, world peace. But today didn't look like it'd be my crowning glory; the funhouse mirror leaned toward the heavy side.

Pot pies, too much Thai and thunder thighs. My fate had been sealed. I prayed for the end of time.

"Let me in," Meredith said, banging on the door.

"Uh-uh, no way." I tugged on first one, and then another. "I'll let you see the ones I like," I promised.

Finally, one labeled as "long torso" seemed to fit. Duh! How come I never thought a long-torso, one-piece suit would be ideal for my 5-foot-3 physique?

I opened the door with reluctance.

"Not bad," Meredith said. "Turn around."

"No," I refused. "I don't like the way it looks from the back." I studied my reflection in the dressing room mirror, which captured every aspect of my derriere. "Or maybe I don't like the way *I* look from the back."

"You could exercise," Meredith advised me as only a twenty-something with a perfect figure could.

"I exercise," I commented. I loved to tease my daughter.

"When?" Meredith asked with a cocked brow.

"Don't you hear the bracelets jingling as I turn the pages when reading every night?" I countered. "It must be helping my arms. And I'm working my stomach muscles now, and almost every day, when I try to hold my tummy in."

Meredith groaned.

"Well, how about a cover-up? Try this sarong," my brilliant daughter offered, handing me an item of redemption.

"Perfect," I said, wrapping the beautiful scarf around my hips. "This will work," I cooed, prancing and preening before the mirror like the old days, much to Meredith's chagrin.

Then brilliance struck this middle-aged beauty, at last happy with herself and her swimsuit selection: "Before it was sa-rong," I joked, "and now it's so right!"

Dressing to Kill is Killing Me

by
Terri Duncan

I used to dread the arrival of swimsuit season. Just the thought of having to find a suit that accentuated the positive and sucked in the negative made me wish I lived in a place of eternal snows and bulky overcoats.

However, I despise the coming of winter just as much, because of the holiday party season. Overall, the holidays are stressful enough, but just when I've convinced myself I can dutifully survive the long lines and steadily mounting charge account balances, the dreaded invitations begin arriving. There are holiday gatherings, festive get-togethers and office galas, all of which call for a different outfit. I find myself spending long hours contemplating the true meaning, not of Christmas, but of holiday casual and festive best. Even the phrase *cocktail attire* makes me shudder. The only cocktail I am accustomed to is the fruited variety found in a can.

My husband simply cannot understand my annual dilemma, when I immerse myself in the world of fashion only to drown amongst the myriad choices. He simply wears the same white shirt and black, flat-front slacks to every holiday party. His most tumultuous decision each year is whether to wear the Santa tie or the more conservative holly berry red tie. If I could be so lucky.

Yes, while friends and family, all festive and full of holiday merriment, travel over the river and through the woods to grandmother's house singing Christmas carols, I am full of something else, something a lady probably shouldn't put in print. For days on end, I wander aimlessly from store to store, on that endless task of finding an outfit that actually fits and is flattering to my figure—or lack thereof. Chipper salesclerks working on commission try their best to ply me with eggnog and spiced cider. Forget that. Where's the wine?

As I fret over my holiday clothing anxieties, presents go unwrapped and the turkey goes unplucked; how can one contemplate dressing and gravy when she has to contemplate dressing herself for all of the upcoming events? My husband suggested I just run out and buy a basic black dress, one that would be suitable for all of our invited occasions. Does he not realize that there is no such thing as a basic black dress, that the existence of such a garment is merely an urban fashion legend? Catalogs, stores and online merchants boast of rack after rack, page after page of so-called basic black dresses that are anything but basic. Do I go short or long, silk or satin, empire waist or fitted? Should I look for a scoop neck, a boat neck or do I dare to plunge? Do I opt for strapless, backless, asymmetrical or form-fitting? Does black really qualify as festive or does festive necessitate sequins and baubles? The decisions are endless, thus causing my mood to become even darker than any basic black dress. Perhaps I should look for chartreuse.

Then, of course, there is the accessorizing dilemma. It is not enough to possess the perfect outfit—one must also acquire matching shoes, a handbag and just enough bling to make every other woman envious. Proper accessorizing naturally leads to even more fashion decisions: if I wear open-toed shoes, am I committing a fashion faux pas by wearing hose, or are sickly, pale bare legs with obvious broken veins really in vogue? Do I wear textured hose, fishnets or barely-there nude? Flats are so much more comfortable, but do I forego comfort in order to elongate my legs with lethal stilettos? Do I purchase a strappy evening bag large enough to actually accommodate necessary items, or do I forego practicality and glossy lips and go for a tiny, dainty clutch that I will surely leave behind since it will not be strapped to my body? If I wear silver slides, must I also wear silver jewelry or is the mixing of precious metals in style this holiday season?

Next—hair. Every year I worry about my mop most people refer to as hair. Does the holiday occasion and the outfit call for an updo by a professional hair dresser, or do I entrust this task to my absolutely incapable hands and multiple cans of hair spray? Do I add festive holiday barrettes or spray on a light sheen of red, green and silver glitter to my tiresome locks? Or do I forego all of this and wear one of those trendy hats that Princess Kate is so fond of . . . you know, one of those jaunty fascinators. If so, what color? What style? Feathers? Beads?

Netting? Satin? Loops? But the most important question is this: will I look as fascinating as Her Royal Highness? And all of this hat talk leads to another dilemma—if I try pulling off a fashionable Kate look, I'll have to rethink my entire outfit and also buy hubby a respectable English tie. Oh, and I'll need some Harry Winston diamond knock-offs as well.

When the holiday attire requirements are met and paid for, the real fear sets in. I worry I will arrive at the party and discover three other women wearing the same outfit! In addition, not only have they accessorized with much more pizzazz, the dress looks better on all three of them than on me! Therefore, in order to deter this from happening, I drive at least 300 miles away from the site of the gathering to purchase my holiday wardrobe, all to ensure I will possess a truly unique and chic dress. This means shopping at outrageously expensive, ritzy boutiques I cannot afford instead of a department store with a beleaguered clearance rack, which is where the contents of my wallet say I should be shopping. And don't get me started on the cost of gasoline these days. The price to fill my tank and make the six-hour trek for the perfect outfit drives up exponentially the cost of outfitting myself. Multiply this by all of the invitations on the refrigerator door, and obtaining a second mortgage is discussed each year.

Now Martha Stewart may be able to transform a tattered green sweat suit, some leftover Christmas decorations and a strand of tinsel into an elegant but comfortable ensemble suitable for any holiday gathering. I am also quite certain that she could manage to accessorize using recycled soup cans, old sneakers, a little hot glue and imagination, but I am not so talented. I fear I will be overdressed, underdressed or totally out-dressed at each and every gathering. No matter what I purchase and resolutely decide upon, rest assured I will change the ensemble and the vast array of outrageously expensive accessories a minimum of three times before the event. My hair will inevitably get mussed in the dressing process and I will get a run in my hose. I will then cry in utter frustration and ruin my carefully applied holiday makeup. Therefore, I will be forced to begin the entire process from scratch and the ordeal will probably cause us to be late to the party, despite the fact I began the process weeks in advance.

Perhaps worst of all, when I finally deem myself presentable, my husband, all decked out in his finest holiday tie, white oxfords and black slacks, will take one look at me and say, "You're wearing *that*?" My response? "Here, honey, let me strangle, I mean straighten, your tie. Oh dear! Is that too tight?"

But this holiday season, things will be different. Very different. Dressing to kill is killing me, and I simply cannot endure this ordeal ever again. Therefore, I have decided to throw my own Christmas shindig and invite each and every one of those who normally send an invitation to us. In this manner, I will fulfill my social obligations in one evening and on my own terms. The invitations are already addressed, stamped and awaiting the mailman. They read: "You are cordially invited to our first annual, clothing-optional holiday luau."

Remember, I don't like swimsuit shopping. But what should I do with my hair?

Terri

Husband Jayson and Terri

CHAPTER
TWO

Worth Our Weight in Gold

And damn, we're worth every penny!

Honey, You're a Fat Ass

by
Terri Spilman

The big day was here. The training. The starving. The planning. After six years of sitting on the sidelines, my head was finally in the game. It was a sweltering day. Our leader was steadily sipping water through a straw from her convenience store gallon-sized tumbler. As I stood nervously in line, it was finally my turn. I took off my shoes and stepped onto the platform. The judge said, "Wow, 6.4!" Yes! I did it. I actually dropped 6 pounds my first week of Weight Watchers.

Let's just say that the perfect storm of giving birth at the age of 41, becoming peri-menopausal and being a stay-at-home mom hasn't exactly been kind to my waistline. Can you say, "M-e-n-o-p-o-t?" Several attempts at getting in shape have failed over the years for one reason or another. So for my birthday, my mother decided to gift me a monthly pass to Weight Watchers. She will tell you the conversation went, "Now don't get mad, but I want you to go to Weight Watchers with me." I heard, "Honey, you're a fat ass."

It is not the easiest thing to tell a loved one that they need to shed a few pounds. A few months ago, we went on a family trip to Rochester, Minnesota—home to the world-famous Mayo Clinic. While browsing in a Barnes and Noble bookstore in the historic Chateau Theatre, my father-in-law casually pointed out a Mayo Clinic Diet book. He said, "I don't mean nothin', but if I needed to go on a diet, this would be a pretty good book." He had also given me his pedometer a few years back; I thought he let me keep it because I had accidentally dropped it in the toilet. I now know it was a big fat hint. OK, a well-intended, big fat hint.

Comments from other loved ones—"You're just a little fat, Mom" and "You have a gait like Tony Soprano"—were starting to take their toll. The final straw was blowing out a pair of my favorite Capri jeans in the thigh area. I'm lucky a small brush fire didn't erupt due to the friction.

This was my third round with Weight Watchers over the years. I guess I have a love/hate relationship, similar to that of Richard Burton and Elizabeth Taylor. You know, you really need each other but you just can't stay loyal. Maybe the third time was the charm because the program seemed much easier to follow.

For all the newbies out there, participants in the program are allocated a certain number of points per day based on calories, fat grams and fiber content. The average person gets 25 to 30 points per day. The backbone of the program requires having to write down everything you put in your mouth and allocate a point total to each item. A new part of that documentation had to do with "BLTs." I thought, *Great! Bacon, lettuce and tomato sandwiches every day.* Not quite. BLT stands for "bite, lick and taste." This was particularly disturbing for the pastry chef attending our meeting. I wished her luck.

Doing some calculations, I figured out I could earn an extra 20 points in food a day if I were a construction worker who was breastfeeding. Furthermore, I could earn extra points just for walking on crutches. Sounds like too much work, but it sure was tempting on the days when the "Salt Fairy" visited.

As you progress through the program, awards are given out for weight lost and milestones met. For every 5 pounds lost, participants earn a paper star. Until recently, ribbons were rewarded for such milestones, but, in an ironic twist, I guess the Weight Watchers folks thought ribbons were too State Fair.

And if you lose the weight and keep it off, you start earning charms. At the end of the program, I'm either going to be cooking s'mores over a bonfire, burning my paper stars in frustration, or be sounding like a building superintendent jiggling my waist full of charms. At least it won't be my ass that is doing the jiggling.

Our leader refers to my mom and me as the "mother-daughter team." Hence, we are the Naomi and Wynonna Judd of our weekly meeting. Our leader asked me to share what my strategy was for dropping my first 5 pounds. I told her I shaved everything before the weigh-in. I literally did. I also said I was even contemplating wearing a paper exam gown just to lighten the load and that it would be the perfect place to stick my paper star. She understood. This is a woman who has lost 67 pounds and carries her pedometer in a plastic bag at an amusement park so it doesn't get soaked on the water rides. That is commitment.

So wish us luck on our adventure. As our leader says, "We'll be seeing less of you next week."

The Revolving Door

by
Elynne Chaplik-Aleskow

I have had a weight problem since I was a child. One of my closest and most cherished friends is chocolate. Even pronouncing the word makes me salivate. Chocolate has been a pure, constant and delicious companion.

My sisters and I all battle the scale. Sugar is our nemesis. My sister Linda and I have an ongoing joke that we have never been thin at the same time. We are always giving each other pep talks about losing weight. We try our hardest to motivate one another without creating resentment or interference with our beloved chocolate.

One winter morning I got on the scale and wept. How did the number I was staring at happen? I swore that I would start my diet that day and would give up chocolate until I reached my goal. To guarantee my promise to myself, I called Linda and said it aloud to her. Now it was real and that made it scary.

To my surprise, four weeks passed and I had not once cheated. I worked downtown and decided one day to do some errands. As I was walking down the main boulevard of Chicago, I suddenly looked up and realized that I was standing, while waiting for the traffic light to change, in front of a Fannie May Candy Store. This was my favorite chocolate in the world next to Cadbury.

As I looked in the window at the display of boxes filled with chocolate butter creams, turtles and fudge, my knees started to buckle. I almost had to hold on to the side of the building. I could feel my resolve dissolving. *One month*, I kept saying to myself. *You have gone without chocolate for one month. Keep walking. Cross the street. NOW!*

But I was not listening to myself. The imagined taste of the chocolate on my tongue had taken over. My brain had disengaged. Only my taste buds were operating in anticipation of what I was about to do.

I walked to the store's revolving door and entered. I pushed hard to make the door go as fast as I could. As the door swung into the store, I was ready to disembark toward the candy counter when I realized that I could not stop revolving and therefore could not enter the store! Somehow the door kept going until I was again outside on the street. I looked up in shock to see my sister Linda behind me pushing that door with all her strength. I had pushed myself into the store and she had pushed me out.

Linda happened to be passing by at the moment I weakened. She saw me start my journey toward chocolate and moved as quickly as she could to save me. And she did. We laughed so hard that my need for a chocolate fix passed for the moment. The next craving was an absolute surety. The question was not if, but when, and where would Linda be when I needed her?!

Size 14 is Not a Curse

by
Mary Horner

Suckered—again!

I had just devoured the magazine article about weight loss with interest, just like I had read all those other magazine articles about weight loss. I wanted to find out how these women lost their 10 or 20 or 30 pounds of ugly fat. And have you ever noticed how they always call it *ugly fat*? I've never seen my own fat, so I don't know if it is ugly or not, but I prefer the term *feminine fat*. Somehow, it suits me. It reminds me of the term *feminine mystique*. And it sure is a *mysterique* how the fat got there in the first place!

It doesn't matter which magazine I read, because similar articles are in all of them. Their headlines jump out at me while I'm in line at the grocery store, usually tired and hungry from a long day at work, the time when I am most susceptible to purchase magazines with headlines like, "How I Lost 100 pounds and Went From a Size 14 to a Size 8."

Oprah did it, Valerie did it, and a lady from Toledo did it. They all went from size 14s to their dream sizes. Some may need to do it again, but that's beside the point. I read them because I am trying to lose 15 to 20 pounds. I want inspiration. I want to have a life like the "after" stories these women have. You know, those who say things like, "I lost weight and look great, can wear anything in my closet and my younger sister's closet, went back to school and got a great job, great salary, great man. And now I feel like I can do anything, even get a good table in a restaurant when I go there alone." In other words, they're living the Good Life, the life that happens to the beautiful people and those who can toss those size 14 clothes right out the window.

"I got my confidence back," one woman told the interviewer as she sat next to her pool in a sleek little black bathing suit, showing off her polished nails and designer hair and matching sunglasses. "After I lost 70 pounds, my kids listen to me and my husband picks up his dirty underwear that used to lay lifeless on the floor for days on end." She said she owed it all to her escape from the curse of size-14 clothes.

I guess it's cultural. Size 14 means you are fat. Size 10 means you are thin. I want to know how these women can lose 70 pounds and go down only two sizes when several weight-loss experts I consulted say people usually drop a size with every 15 pounds or so. Could these former full-bodied femme fatales be stretching the truth, or do they shop at stores whose sizing standards are somewhat liberal? I hope so, because I am 5-foot-6-inches tall and weigh a 100 and plenty. Guess what size that means? You guessed it, the dreaded size 14. The same size the fat lady in the circus wears.

Yes, I admit freely that a 10- or 20-pound loss would be welcomed, and I work at it. But in the meantime, I'm comfortable at this weight. I exercise and eat well and have energy and (some) stylish clothes that fit when I get around to doing the laundry. (OK, I know if I lost the weight and was a size 10 I would probably have a maid to do the laundry.) But in the meantime, why am I lumped in with the obese? I'll tell you why. Because some 5-foot-2-inch woman who weighed 185 pounds said her fat clothes were a size 14.

I don't begrudge those who have more weight to lose than I. I empathize with them. I feel for them. I listen to their stories and realize I am only a few Christmas feasts, or half a year or so of bad PMS months, away from the weights showing on their scales. I don't have some of the stresses they do, but I also have some they don't. I'm not saying either one of us is better or worse, more happy or sad; we are just not the same size. So why am I wearing their clothes?

Maybe I'm going about this the wrong way. Maybe I need to find out where they shop! Maybe they shop in stores that have buyers who have a few pounds to lose themselves and buy clothes from manufacturers whose tags reflect anything above a size 12—no matter how large—as a size 14.

Where would I find this information? Who will tell me? I have friends who are heavier than me, but they never mention it. I've even gone shopping with them, and not a word was spoken. Well, I'm on to them and my mission is clear: I'll stalk them at the mall, I'll scour the department stores to find the right sales clerk who will lead me to the land of One Size 14 Fits All. Maybe a secret password is all I need. One thing's for sure, now I know why the salesclerks look like they are sharing a secret . . . they are.

Until I find someone willing to talk, I think there ought to be a law about truth in adver*sizing*!

Got Love Handles?

by
Donna Collins Tinsley

As a young girl, I remember hearing about "love handles" and wondering what the heck they were. Skinny as I was, there was no way to pinch an inch of flesh on me.

Later in my life, before I married my husband Bill, I got up at 5:30 each morning and jogged, all in an effort to keep my girlish figure. But after we were married, Bill said to me, "I didn't wait 26 years to get married to wake up alone in the morning." What a guy! It was hard to give up that morning run, but as the Good Book says, "Fit in with your husband's plans." I wanted to be a good wife. And with that, my morning jog dropped off my daily agenda.

Wanting to keep some type of morning health routine going, I switched to sit-ups. When I complained about aching shoulders, Bill commented, "It's probably because you keep jumping out of bed to do them without warming up." I gave up sit-ups.

It didn't take long for me to notice strange things happening to my body when I put on my swimsuit: there were new bulges, skin hanging loosely and, oh no—love handles!

It was Bill's fault, plain and simple. But should I be mad at my dear husband or at all those great looking women on the cover of every magazine newsstand? Who said women in their 50s had to have abs of steel? I remember when Jane Fonda came on the scene with her exercise videos—the claim was that every woman could look young, supple and lean if she followed Jane's lead. I tried and could never do the whole video, but I really felt healthy as I watched her workout.

It used to be the accepted norm for a woman in her 50s to sit on a porch swing, drink iced tea and look matronly. But those days are over. Now we have Oprah, Goldie Hawn, Demi Moore, Ann-Margret (I swear, that woman never ages) and countless others in their 50s and beyond, looking like schoolgirls.

And then there were the Dove body soap ads with nude women, all over age 50, brandished on billboards all across the country! Yes, these women, who came in a wide variety of sizes, had nearly every square inch of their nakedness splayed across those large outdoor canvases for the world to see. I wondered what their grandchildren thought? One thing I did notice, however, after that initial showing, was that Dove switched and once again ran ads with the most youthful looking ladies, anyway. Maybe America really didn't want to see people who reminded them of their mothers or grandmothers in the nude?

I can cite hundreds of more examples of how society thinks 50-plus-year-old women are supposed to look, but I have better things to do than pen the great American novel. And yes, it would be a fiction. Instead, I want it on record that I protest and challenge the social norms set upon us Baby Boomer ladies! Let us look the way we want to look, and I say, "If you don't like it, you can lump it!" That's an old Southern saying that doesn't make much sense, but Mama used to say it to us all the time.

My darling husband began to notice that the exercise advice he gave me—you know, that advice *not* to exercise when we first got married—was probably not the best advice after all. So he bought me one of those fancy exercise machines, the one that works every inch of your body. And, the manufacturer claimed, it would only take a few minutes a day. Not thrilled with his surprise, I got the supreme revenge; I let that expensive machine sit on the back porch and rust. Now the poor man is afraid to buy me handheld exercise weights, even though I asked him to put some in my stocking for Christmas.

When *I* decided it was time to do something about the shape my body was in, the two of us took out a membership to the YMCA. On my first day, I saw people older than me on the exercise machines and equipment, doing way more than I could ever hope to master.

Seeing this made me too embarrassed to ask for help learning the many workout machines. Instead, I hopped onto a treadmill, a safe bet in my mind, because all I would be doing was walking. But evidently I'm not really good at walking with something moving beneath me. Trying to distract myself from the boredom from endless walking, I watched the television set directly above me. When my show went to commercial, I tried to watch another show playing four televisions away. I kept backing up to see it and the next thing I knew, I fell sideways onto the treadmill beside mine. Jumping up immediately, with the only thing hurt being my dignity, I heard an older fellow, in good control of his machine, ask, "Are you OK?" I nodded sheepishly. For the rest of my workout, I hung on for dear life to the treadmill's handles.

I canceled my membership at the YMCA after that.

You know, I'm finding that Bill's love is handling my "love handles" pretty good. He says, "Look at the women in the paintings by the great artists—they all have well defined stomachs." So I guess the next phase of my life will be as a model for Renaissance paintings.

Any of y'all out there with love handles want to join me in this? I bet we will make more money than all the Dove ads put together!

Zigzagging

by
Caroleah Johnson

I have a box of clothes from the 1970s on the top shelf of my closet. I don't know why I keep them other than an undying sense of optimism that makes me think I will someday be a size 10 again. But after losing nearly 300 pounds, I've decided to quit dieting. That's not really an impressive amount of weight loss if you consider it's the same 30 pounds I've lost ten times now.

I've zigzagged back and forth between sizes like the rickrack that used to adorn clothes in times past. I'm ready to end my 40-year, love-hate relationship with the bathroom scales. I'm not getting any younger and I'm tired of storing four different sizes of clothes in my closet: my fat-size clothes, my not-quite-so-fat-size clothes, my almost-down-to-goal-size clothes and the only-in-my-dreams-size clothes.

For all of my lack of success in conquering the weight issue, I figure I have made a significant contribution to the weight loss industry over the years. My bookshelves are sagging under the weight of my extensive collection of diet books. It looks more like an international travel section from the library: There is the *South Beach Diet*, *The Hollywood Diet*, *The Mediterranean Diet* and *The Okinawa Diet*, to mention a few. I have books touting low carbs, high carbs, no fat, lots of fat, no fiber, huge amounts of fiber, no meat, all meat, no dairy, raw dairy and numerous other variations. I have books promising me weight loss in 30 days, in 10 days, in eight minutes and even one minute.

It seems that anyone who has ever lost weight can write a book promoting their plan. And there will always be people as optimistic as I am who will buy those books. I've plunked down plenty of hard-earned cash for them, thinking that because it worked for somebody, it would work for me. But in the end, all I lost was a few more dollars. I'm actually considering boxing up all these books and opening my own used bookstore.

No, I no longer diet. I'm not interested in the latest weight-loss scheme. I haven't resigned myself to waddling through my remaining years, but I have finally realized that dieting involves a frame of mind that sets oneself up for certain failure. And I've also learned other important facts, such as that thinness does not necessarily equate to healthiness. You can be healthy and still be overweight or you can be thin and be very unhealthy. Skin hides a lot. I've learned there's a direct connection between what I eat and how I feel. Why didn't a doctor ever tell me that? I've learned that one bad day doesn't have to derail a healthy eating plan and one hot fudge sundae is not an excuse for a three-day binge. I've also learned that grandchildren like a lap that has a little cushioning and bony knees aren't comfortable for sleeping on without some padding between them.

I'm not grossly overweight, but I know that a substantial amount of weight loss at this point in life will only leave me with more droopy skin and goodness knows, I don't need more wrinkles. I'm healthy and have blood work to prove it, I still have a fair amount of energy, and I look reasonably good in the right clothes. While it's true I don't have the body I had at age 30, I'm not bemoaning that. It was hard to maintain that body. The important thing is that I'm finally comfortable with the woman I am, even if I do pack a few extra pounds.

And those size 10 clothes on the top shelf of my closet? I'm sure they are no longer in style anyway. Perhaps I'll see if there's a market for retro clothes on eBay. Someone must want a brown pantsuit trimmed with yellow rickrack.

It's Gotta Be the Hair

by

Mary-Lane Kamberg

My first hint that I needed a new hairstyle came one cold winter day when I was shopping at the mall. I'd been wearing my hair the same way for years, ever since I told Greg, my hairstylist, that I wanted a short, easy-care 'do. After all, I was a busy career mom with no time for fussing with gel or a curling iron.

"I want to wash my hair, and then drive 70 mph down the interstate with the sunroof open," I told him. He complied with a short cut, parted to the side. I loved it. And since then I returned once a month for a trim—that is, until the crisis that catapulted me back to the salon for a makeover.

I was looking at sweaters at the Gap, when a teenage girl approached me and asked, "May I help you, sir?"

I looked around. *Did she mean me?*

"Oh, I'm so sorry," she said when she got a closer look.

"That's OK" I said. "I'm just looking."

No problem, I thought. At 5-feet-8, I'm on the tall side for a woman. And I was wearing a bulky coat.

Later, when I told my sister what happened, she reassured me. "No, you don't look like a man. It's gotta be the hair. It's pretty short."

"You're right," I said. "And I wasn't wearing earrings or makeup."

Having sufficiently rationalized the situation, I resumed my routine. But it happened again—not once, but twice! Two more strangers called me "sir."

"My hair is too short!" I told Greg at my next appointment. "Three different people called me, 'sir!'"

Greg laughed. In the mirror I noticed the beautician at the next workstation hide a smile. She had mid-length hair with a perky flip. No one would ever mistake her gender.

"I'm serious," I said, ignoring Ms. Perky. "Leave it a little longer this time," I instructed Greg. He shaped my hair accordingly, stifling occasional chuckles.

A couple of weeks later, my day once again was ruined when a server at my favorite restaurant asked, "What can I get you, sir?"

I freshened my lipstick.

"At least it only happened once this time," I said, as Greg draped a plastic cape over my shoulders. "But I need a more feminine style."

Greg chuckled. I glared at him, and he attempted a more concerned look. "What do you have in mind?"

I glanced around the salon and spotted another beautician wearing a style I liked. "How about that?"

Greg studied the hairdo—a layered look with long bangs,

feathered sides and spiky wisps on top. "You'll have to use gel and hairspray or it won't stay," he advised.

"I don't care. Go for it."

In the weeks after the appointment, I attended meetings, went shopping and had dinner with relatives. Not a single soul called me "sir." I was thrilled.

Soon after, a friend and I met at a local restaurant for lunch. She greeted me with much enthusiasm. "Have you lost weight?" she asked, as we hugged. "You look great!"

I shook my head. My weight hadn't changed. But thinking of my hero Greg, I had to smile. I couldn't wait to tell him that he had not only made me look more feminine, he had also created what I was sure would become the latest craze and his new specialty: "The World-Famous, Weight-Loss Haircut!"

High Five

by
Alice Muschany

On my 30th birthday, I received an unexpected present, and it didn't come in a pretty box wrapped with satin. Without increasing my intake of calories or fat grams, an extra 5 pounds appeared on my thighs. "Where did that come from?" I asked the chubby girl staring back at me in the mirror.

Since that first "gift" at age 30, I've tried every diet trick available. One popular magazine swore drinking ice water all day would melt away pound after pound, but all I got were the chills. Next I tried using a smaller plate and wondered if going back for seconds counted as exercise. Drinking green tea to speed up my metabolism only sped up my trips to the bathroom. And the grapefruit diet? Forget that. It only turned me into a sourpuss. Exhausting all other avenues, I finally joined a weight-loss group, but after three weeks, all I lost was 21 days.

Just like clockwork, when my 40th birthday rolled around, another 5 pounds magically appeared on my backside. And despite that pull of gravity, I didn't take it sitting down! I began lifting weights and lengthened my daily walk. One glamour magazine advised not to eat after six in the evening. That formula only worked if I beefed up dinner. The cabbage diet came with a warning: "This diet should not be followed for more than seven days at a time." No problem there. On day four, I went ape over bananas since the diet allowed up to eight daily. At least I got a little exercise swinging from a tree.

Those extra 5 pounds at age 45 caught me totally off-guard. *What happened to my 10-year grace period?* I wondered. *Is this what I have to look forward to? A pound a year for life?* I switched to power walking and pumped my arms like a drum majorette, the only result being tennis elbow.

"Boot camp," a girlfriend suggested.

Why not? Something had to give, and if things didn't change, it would be my elastic waistband. After two weeks of aerobic exercise, all I lost was pride. Face it, spandex didn't look quite the same on me as it did on the 20-year-olds.

When the BIG five-oh reared its ugly head, the scale registered another 5 pounds, which generously included my middle this time, not just my saddlebags. *What's up with that?* I added wrist and ankle weights to my workout and purchased a talking bathroom scale that announced my weight in a pleasant female voice.

At 55, the scale blabbed another 5 pounds. "Shut up!" I yelled as I kicked it across the room. If I even looked at food or drooled over a commercial, my numbers climbed higher. And snacking? Gooey butter cakes and potato chips—forever on my hips. I switched to 10-pound weights and purchased a Stairmaster.

I only have a two-year waiting period to discover what my next over-the-hill, five-more-years birthday will bestow upon me. But rumor has it, a person's metabolism speeds up after age 60.

Hooray! Thin is just around the corner! I'll have fries with that!

Happy birthday, Alice!

Starve Yourself Thin

by
Marijo Herndon

Most diet programs promise the same thing: "Fast and Easy Weight Loss." All I know is that it's never fast. It's certainly not easy, and the fact that I haven't been able to see my feet since the late 1970s showcases my level of determination.

After failing miserably on so many diets, I've become very distrustful of anyone telling me that I can eat whatever I want and not feel deprived. How am I supposed to believe those people on television when they tell me they didn't feel hungry while losing 110 pounds? I'm sorry, but in order to lose that kind of weight, I would imagine there's a whole lot of hungry going on.

Deprivation was always at the forefront of all the diets I've tried. I've attempted Weight Watchers, Diet Workshop, LA Weight Loss, counting calories, counting carbohydrates, counting protein, even the cabbage-soup diet—not my personal favorite for obvious reasons.

And while on every one of them, I found myself watching the clock in anticipation of that next tiny morsel of broccoli to be followed by a bucket of water, all meant to satisfy my hunger. Yum! Not.

I have to admit, I did enjoy going to the Weight Watchers meetings, because the leaders always seemed to be so cheerful and perky talking about all those points you get to eat. The first I heard of this, I said, "How does one eat a point? What are these points you speak of?" When I found out it was a system of counting food, I got so excited when I heard I could have 26 points, until I realized that 26 points is barely enough food to sustain a hummingbird. OK, secretly, I wanted to slap every one of them (the leaders, not the hummingbirds), but while I was there listening to them talk, they made me feel like I could be like them—thin and energetic. Of course, I would have to eat like them, exercise and tell myself I liked counting points because it was fun! There was a problem. I didn't like it. And it wasn't nearly as much fun as they made it sound.

One leader had the nerve to say, "Every time you count a point, an angel sings." But I didn't want to count points. I wanted a Snickers. I didn't want to use the stair stepper at the gym like they told us to. I wanted to stay home and watch the Food Network on TV. I could make an exhilarating game of guessing how many points are in one of Paula Deen's dishes. Or I could dream of what it might be like to be Guy Fieri, traveling to all those *Diners, Drive-Ins and Dives*. Honestly, Paula and Guy make me feel cheerful and energetic and aren't those the real *points* in life?

There are only a few diets that I haven't tried, because I

don't believe they tell you the truth. I would regain, at least, some modicum of faith in the diet industry if, just once, they would come out and say, "You will feel dizzy, famished and irritable until you eat cake." Now *that's* a program I could trust.

I can remember watching Kirstie Alley melt away the pounds on commercial after commercial for Jenny Craig. She kept saying, "It's so easy." The first commercial didn't even show her bottom half because of its apparent size. And within weeks, she was shown dancing in the street and getting thrown 15 feet in the air by svelte, young men. Come on, Jenny, do you really think we're going to buy that as truth? This takes deception to a whole new level. And I've never actually seen hide nor hair of Ms. Jenny Craig. For all I know she is, in reality, an aging, bald fat man.

Dr. Atkins swore that his diet would keep us all healthy and living well into our 90s. "You'll always feel full," he said. Lots of red meat, bacon, eggs, cream and cheeses were the staple of his plan, all the while depriving us of a mere grain of rice. However, I'll never know how long he would have lived. To think the man spent an entire lifetime warding off carbohydrates like the plague, and in the end, it wasn't a crouton that killed him but a nasty bump on the head sustained during a fall. I'll bet you an apple pie that he didn't slip on the ice, but on a puddle of bacon grease. I have to wonder if on his way down he didn't yell out for a baked potato. And it didn't matter whether he ate rye bread or a flank steak because the only thing that would have prolonged his life was in actuality, a helmet. If only someone had told him he would be weak and lightheaded from dieting, he might still be alive today. To be on the safe side, whenever I eat bacon, I'm wearing a helmet.

I love the name "South Beach Diet." Just hearing the words *south* and *beach* gives me a warm, fuzzy feeling. It also gives me the illusion that one day I'll be able to wear a string bikini. (For any of you who know me, I'll pause here for you to gain your composure.) Dr. Agatston, the founder (mind you, his name sounds a lot like Atkins, so already I'm suspicious) brags, "You won't have any cravings." You also won't have any bread, rice, cereal, fruit or potatoes for the first 14 days of the plan. Now, when you tell a fat woman she can't have a potato for 14 days, you better slap a helmet on her, because she's going down.

Enough of this, I say! I have so much experience trying to lose weight that I'm going to start my own diet program. I'm calling it "Starve Yourself Thin." It's honest and to the point. No games here! Let's face it; I've done enough of them to know how they work. My truthful marketing campaign will attract veteran dieters, since surely, they must be sick of all the deceptions, too. And I will post a full disclosure for newcomers, so they are aware of what they are getting themselves into:

- You will feel deprived because you will eat the tiniest portions of green food, made to look like real food of other colors.
- This plan will not be fun. We cannot stress this enough.
- You will not have to count points or anything else, for that matter. With the amount of food you will eat, your thinking will be fogged.
- When you prepare the tiniest of meals for yourself,

you will raise your arms to the heavens, with fists of might, and yell, "Why God? Why?" (Raising arms is optional, as you won't have much strength.)

- You will have to prepare separate meals for your family because they will threaten you with bodily harm if you serve them your cauliflower leek puree and try to pass it off as a decadent cream sauce.

- As you watch the rest of your family eat burgers, mashed potatoes and bagels, you will seethe with resentment.

- The only exercise you will have strength for is Seething with Resentment. (Yes, resentment is an exercise and instructions will be on your diet sheet.)

- Whenever you hear a diet spokesperson profess you can feel great, eat whatever you want and lose weight, you will repeat the mantra, "YOU ARE A BIG FAT LIAR."

- We here at Starve Yourself Thin are all about exposing the truth. We pull no punches here, because we just don't have the energy.

- Sign up NOW and receive your free Starve-Yourself-Thin helmet engraved with our motto: "To tell you the truth, I'm starving!"

Now this is a diet I can believe in. Call Jenny? I don't think so!

CHAPTER THREE

They're Called Boobs!

Need we say more?

Tan Lines

by
Susan Nickerson

The colors of the morning were so vibrant, I swear I heard them breathe as Peter and I ambled across the golden grains of sand. We stood at water's edge as the tide lapped our toes, tickled our souls and washed away our troubles. Lush silence rendered us speechless; we exchanged words with our eyes. *Paradise. Heaven. Nirvana.*

Palm trees fringed our hidden cove. Their graceful fronds offered slices of shade where we took refuge from the sultry sun. We dined on exotic fruits, sipped papaya wine and unwound in total bliss. A perfect tropical picnic in the warm embrace of the Virgin Islands.

While nodding off on my oversized towel, I was feeling a bit self-conscious about the extra skin on my tummy, even though we were totally alone. It got me thinking about other women I'd seen on the island, prancing about in just Coppertone and thongs, their brown breasts bouncing freely. Some of them had extra skin. Some even had handfuls of it. They didn't care one bit. So why was I so excessively uncomfortable? *What am I missing?* I thought. *I can certainly go topless. Or can I?*

Forever shielded from the rays of the sun, my two delicate white ladies were a bit shy—frightened, if you will. But the hypnotic fragrance of wild jasmine, ever present in the balmy breeze, along with a belly full of wine, gave me the intoxicated courage I needed and off came my top. I slid my eyes towards Peter expecting some type of reaction—a lewd whistle per- haps—but the wine and heat had already knocked him out.

I stood up straight and faced the water then turned back toward the beach to assure my girls that we were all safe. Clearly, we had no experience in unity without the support of cups, so as one swung east, the other swung west, and my extra skin headed north. Once we all settled down and learned how to walk as one, we headed toward the sea. Along the way I showed them the clouds. They felt the warmth of the sun's rays, yet neither one seemed impressed, wondering what the benefits of being free would yield. "How about no tan lines, ladies?" They perked right up.

I'd done it! I was topless! *You go girl, you be jammin', you be steamin'.* I was so proud. *I want to swim, float and frolic with the dolphins. I'm an island girl, a hula dancer, Jane of the jungle.* I grabbed my snorkel gear and shuffled into the water singing, "Hey, Mr. Tallyman, tally THESE . . ." *Wait, my girls don't look like bananas,* I thought. Then I had it—I ended the line with "coconuts."

I followed schools of bright, green parrotfish while they

munched on coral and I dove for unusual shells that I slipped into my bathing suit bottoms for safe keeping. The ladies sloshed about, clumsy at first. They tried to split up and swim solo, so I surfaced until we could regroup. I drifted for a while and it was wonderful. My skin started to wrinkle. The girls pooped out and flung themselves overboard, but still I drifted.

As the wine began to wear off, I felt a strange, stinging sensation in the *nippular* area so I headed toward shore, hoping no sea creatures had mistaken us for bait. It was then I saw them. People. On our deserted beach. In our paradise. People. Lots and lots of them.

Colorful umbrellas dotted the landscape, towels and sand chairs had been scattered about like a scene from *Beach Blanket Bingo*. Trapped in the water with my naked girls, I frantically ducked under the water as I tried to plot my escape. Coughing and gasping for air, I emerged from the once tranquil sea with my mask, snorkel and soggy breasts. I tried to remove my big awkward flippers but fell back, bottom-heavy, into the sea. My rather large seashell collection had shifted south.

Determined to rise with dignity, I stretched out my suit bottoms and tried to shimmy the shells free, but the sudden clacking sound turned every face toward the giant castanet. I was no longer an exotic island girl. No Jane of the jungle here. I was Ursula, the 500-pound sea witch emerging from her underwater lair, irritable all the way from my middle-aged spread down to my butt full of grit.

Peter rushed to my rescue with his scratchy, sand-covered towel, but the girls winced when he wrapped it around us. We had eluded the sea creatures, but it stung to see my badly sunburned girls, hanging low in shame. I wished I had thought about sun block. Or brought a kicky little seashell bag that I could hang around my neck so as not to scare the perky little Gidgets that spilled out of another Carnival Cruise van. I swear I heard them giggle as I brushed the sand off my red-hot-ladies, adjusted my shells, and waddled onto shore.

"Well, girls," I said, "look at the bright side. At least we won't have any tan lines."

The view from the beach.

Booby Trapped

by
Erika Hoffman

When the technician slid one of my womanly assets onto the glass, she said, "I'm going to compress you a little. This may hurt." She tightened the screw on the apparatus. As it squeezed my lone appendage, I thought of my waffle-making machine and subsequent smashed white batter.

"Yow-eee!" I uttered, closing my eyes tight. "Doesn't the Geneva Convention apply here?"

She didn't crack a smile. "Now, let me move you over some to get a better picture of this area." This Silly-Putty part of me was spread out like a jellyfish on a slide. Down came the instrument of torture. "You'll feel some pressure," she casually remarked. I instantly thought of an old-fashioned lemon juicer. The adage, "When life gives you lemons, make lemonade" did not apply, at least not at this very moment.

"Oweee-ouch!" I wondered to myself if women ever fainted

during mammograms. *Do they simply dangle, held up only by their feminine, amorphous accoutrement which was still pressed like a hydrangea between the pages of a dictionary?* I thought. Finally, my tormentor released me. My squashed breast slithered off the leveling machine. "Phew!" I said, thankful it was still attached.

"One more picture," Marquis de Sade's descendant announced, without remorse. My eyes widened. This time she penned blue dots on my right bosom, trying to pinpoint a particular patch. She studied the Band-Aid she'd earlier placed over my nipple.

"What's the Band-Aid for?" I asked.

"We use it as a guide. We measure from there."

"It's sort of a North Pole navigating device, right?" I countered, trying to lighten the mood in the room, trying to get my tormentor to at least smile. A part of me so wanted her to show me some empathy, something—*anything*! I couldn't imagine she took pleasure from all of this, or she would have smiled, at least a little.

But she didn't respond and instead brought the rack down on me. *Squish.* Flat-ironed again! When she lifted the device and let my maltreated flesh escape, my deflated breast and I made a dash to shed the gown and flee her chamber of horrors.

Meanwhile, she scrutinized the images. "It's probably just a shadow. I'll be right back." She zipped out. Before I could gather my parts together into their respective harnesses, she returned. "We're going down the hall to have an ultrasound done," she said nonchalantly.

"*We?*" *You mean ME! Oh crap*, I thought to myself.

"Do you want to wear the gown?" she asked.

"Do I ever," I muttered sarcastically as I undressed once again and slipped back into the flimsy piece of paper material. The technician escorted me to my next destination and as she turned to leave, she smiled. *Maybe she meant well after all?* I mused, secretly directing the comment to my breasts.

Once in the ultrasound room, I was greeted by a different technician, and a very pleasant one at that. *What a change!* She instructed me to lie on the examining table. We made small talk as she swept her wand all over one side of my chest. The slightly cold tool probed around the surface of my limp mammary gland. This was a picnic after my Gitmo experience, a day at the beach sunning myself, only with more of me exposed. And she was doodling an Etch A Sketch, using my boob as the canvas. When I played with the toy as a kid, I never thought about drawing body parts, or, at least, I'll never own up to it!

She commented on the white spots. "They could be cysts or maybe fatty tissue."

"My mother had cysts. The docs aspirated them," I responded.

"They come back, so that's not done anymore," this nice lady said. "Do you take hormone replacement therapy?"

"Yes."

"Do you like it?"

"I feel better with it. Should I stop taking it?"

"Not if you like it."

The radiologist arrived and after introductions, he pointed at the pictures. They were black negatives with no backlight to illuminate them. I saw nothing.

"They could be cysts," he said while peering into the blackness of the image.

I nodded, absorbing this important fact.

"Or fatty deposits," he added, stroking his chin. "Or nothing, really. Come back in six months for another mammogram to see if they're still there."

"OK."

"Or, how about in three months?" he said, obviously changing his mind, midstream.

"OK . . . "

"But, six months will most likely be fine."

I shook his hand goodbye and thought, in absolute frustration, *Is this why they say "Medicine is an art" because nothing seems definite. Three months? Six? How about four or five?* I felt the doctor was shuffling cards and playing the game of Hearts. The next time the deck was cut and the hand distributed, I hoped I didn't wind up with the Queen of spades.

Getting a mammogram doesn't rate on my list of Top Ten Favorite Things To Do. Nevertheless, they say it's less painful than getting Angelina's puffy lips. And look at all the old Joan Rivers-types running around with bee-stung lips! If the Geritol crowd can suffer that kind of pain for the sake of beauty and wear their badges of courage right out there—completely exposed on their fish faces—surely I can withstand a little pulling, tugging, squeezing, squishing and embarrassment for the sake of my health. Right?

Yet, if any pontificating male declares, "Getting a mammogram is nothing," ask him how he thinks it'll feel when his little pal gets chewed up in a stuck zipper then someone slams a heavy drawer on it and holds that drawer closed for what seems like an eternity! Then the sadist-at-hand follows up his treatment with the farewell remark—while smiling, of course—"Come back and we'll do it again in a couple of months."

I know what I would say: "Gentleman first!"

Everything's Bigger in Texas

by
Kendra Alvey

The shorts were ugly, the wings were greasy, but the tips were supposedly good and I was getting desperate for books and beer money. No more shoveling popcorn or mopping floors. I was getting a real job.

The day of my interview, the place was dead. It was three in the afternoon and the only customers were an older guy in a suit sitting at the bar and two college guys checking out merchandise near the door. As I passed the guys, I could feel their eyes on me. I figured a fully-clothed girl in Hooters was a rare sight.

I walked up to the bar and sat down three chairs over from the suit. After a couple of minutes, a tall blond girl appeared from out of nowhere. I couldn't help but stare. I was eye-level with her chest. Boobs like that were not common in my dorm, and I felt myself wondering if my own would make the cut.

She swung her hair over one shoulder and started playing

with the ends. "Do you have an interview or what?"

"Um, yes. I'm Kendra. My interview's with Donald."

"Hi, Kendra. I'm Jen. I'll go get him." She started to walk off, and then spun around, all blond hair and flying boobs. "I almost forgot—do you want a Diet Coke?"

"Yeah, sure," I said, slowly realizing that the uniform in front of me would be what I'd be required to wear. The tight white tank top, the tiny shiny orange shorts. And, what was with the owl peering at me from the front of the tank top? He was creepy. My mouth was getting really dry. Why did she assume I'd want Diet? Did I look fat? Maybe all Hooters' girls drank Diet.

Jen poured my drink then pranced off to get the manager. I noticed the back of her shirt. It said, "Delightfully tacky, yet unrefined" in brown print. Well, it was certainly tacky. I pictured the miniscule outfit on my own body. My posture suddenly improved. I sucked in my stomach and stuck my chest out. My shoulders were quickly drawn back as if two invisible hands had yanked them from behind.

I'd never really thought about my boobs before. You'd think I would've at least given them a thought, considering I was applying at Hooters, but I hadn't. I guess I was confident to the point of delusion. I knew my boobs weren't small or huge. I knew what size bra I wore, and that guys liked cleavage, but I'd never really thought about how mine measured up. Suddenly I had a lot to think about and not long to do it.

The suit at the end of the bar turned to face me. "You wanna be a Hooters girl, huh?"

I smiled at him. "No, I'm addicted to wings."

He shrugged and took a gulp of beer. "Smart ass, huh? I guess I could see it. I'd have to see you in the uniform."

Apparently Donald had the same idea. After an uneventful interview, he informed me that we'd give it a go. I found out later that this was called "the uniform test." He headed to the back and picked out a small tank and extra small dolphin shorts. I assumed they were called dolphin shorts because of the Miami Dolphins or something, but I didn't ask because I had other issues to worry about. The shorts in his big hands looked like they would fit my old Cabbage Patch Doll.

"I think I'm more like a medium in those," I said, laughing.

"Trust me," he said. "Extra small is better."

Then he outlined the rules. No ponytails or clips. Hair always down and styled. Tan hose under the dolphin shorts. Always have an extra pair. If you are on the floor with a run, you will be sent home. Never wear your uniform outside of work and always change before you leave. And, most importantly, always make sure your makeup is pristine. Oh, and have fun.

Sure. It sounded like a blast.

Before I could fill out my W2 and hiring forms, I had to try the uniform on to make sure it "worked." I felt very self-conscious putting the shorts on. As I stood in front of the mirror sizing up my ass, two girls with identical long, straight blond hair walked into the bathroom.

"Woo-hoo! Lookin' good. Are you new?" the shorter blonde girl asked.

"Yeah, I'm Kendra," I said, knowing my face was red.

"Hi. I'm Alex and this is Brandi," she said, gesturing with her head toward the taller of the two.

Brandi looked me up and down. "Trying them on for the first time, huh?" She walked behind me and grabbed the bottom of the shirt. "Tie it like this and it looks better."

It did. "Thanks."

"Oh, and don't worry, you'll look better once you have hose on and a tan. Cut the bottoms of the hose off, more comfy. Your socks will cover them," Alex added.

She was right. I needed a tan. And more makeup, from the look of these girls. I felt conspicuously pale and self-conscious of my long brown curly hair.

I checked out the two girls as they applied makeup in the mirror. Tight white tank tops revealing mega-cleavage. The brown owl and the orange Hooters' symbol stretched across their large chests like beacons. The orange shorts rode up to reveal quite a glimpse of butt cheek. The hose were deep tan and the shoes and socks spotless white. *At least my feet would be comfortable,* I thought.

Alex and Brandi began a heated discussion about how one of the girls was scandalously pregnant. Their concern was that she would be fat with stretch marks after delivering and would miss her chance at the calendar that year. They didn't seem concerned to me. More like delighted.

Uncomfortable with the topic, I thanked Alex and Brandi for their help and went to find Donald.

The uniform test involved me rotating slowly while Donald eyeballed me in the uniform. I felt not unlike one of the hot dogs I detested, rotating away at the movie theatre. "Looks good," he said and that was that.

By the time I left Hooters, clutching my paperwork, which

was bigger than the uniform, my head was spinning. These girls were straight out of the pages of *Playboy*. Being cute had suddenly gotten way more complicated. I reminded myself that the big tips in my future far outweighed the small shorts.

I called my boyfriend to tell him the good news and to complain about my dilemma. The reaction I got shocked me. He was beyond excited. He was dating a Hooters girl! Ye-freaking-hah! You'd think I'd just been crowned queen of the Dallas Cowboy Cheerleaders and gotten a lifetime supply of beer. I was happy that he was proud of me, but also a little freaked out. Is this what he wanted me to be? Surely he knew I was just doing it for the money. Right?

Before my first training shift, the blond girl's words wouldn't stop echoing in my brain. It was clear that my first shift couldn't begin with me as a white blob, so I got a tanning membership and started tanning. New makeup was also in order. I didn't want to be the sore thumb at Hooters. It was just a matter of time before they discovered I was an imposter and booted me out on my naturally pale ass anyway.

I found that serving the wings was the easy part. The challenge was talking to the other girls. As a theater major, I was used to talking about plays, movies or music. But these girls were different. The discussions made my brain glaze over and my soul shrink. From acrylic nails to highlights, we covered all arenas of primping. I thought the first girls I met at my interview were giving me advice just to be nice, but I soon learned that that's all they talked about. Audrey told me I could iron my hair to get rid of my unsightly curls. Stephie even claimed that if I kept ironing it every night, eventually it would just stay that way. I think she truly believed it, too. Of course, she also believed that American football came before European football, that "they stole the name from us." Aimee showed me how to put blush in my cleavage to make my boobs look bigger, something I was getting a lot of advice on.

After my first day, I bought a push-up bra. By the time I was done training, I had French-tipped acrylic nails and had even learned to open a Diet Coke with them on. Diet Coke became my drink of choice. A month in, my long brown hair had blond highlights. Slowly, I was beginning to feel like one of the gang. My tips were improving and I now had something to talk about with the other girls between rushes.

I was learning how to talk to men, too. The straightforward banter I was used to just didn't cut it. These guys wanted to flirt. So I flirted. And so did they. Hooters was like an alternate universe where guys could say whatever they wanted. I heard comments such as, "You know, I prefer nat'ral titties and yours are lookin' good" or "They should call this place 'Booties' by the look of yours." The strangest thing was not that they made the comments, but that I was OK with it. I would laugh it off. If a guy in my dorm made a remark like that he'd meet the back of my hand, but at work it was fine. I came to expect and even relish the compliments. I guess I figured it meant I was being a good Hooters girl. I now plead temporary insanity brought about by too much bleach.

Outside of work, I was beginning to see that my wardrobe did not fit my new look. I bought more skirts and dresses to show off my tan. I began dressing up for class instead of wearing T-shirts and jeans. My friends must've thought I'd lost my mind. Maybe I had.

My boyfriend was super appreciative of the physical changes. He had a few ideas about some other improvements.

"So, how many of the other girls have fake boobs?" he asked nonchalantly.

"All of them. Why?"

He shrugged. "You ever think about it?"

I hit him on the arm. "No!"

The subject was dismissed, but he'd hit a nerve. I had thought about it. How could I not? I felt like the oddball in the Sesame Street song *Which One of These Things is Not Like the Others*. Even with the tan and highlights, there was still a glaring difference between the blonde-brigade and myself.

The other girls acted like the surgery was no big deal. It was a common subject at work, especially with me, because of my conspicuously natural set. I was shocked by the variety of options. You could go through the bellybutton or under the breast. You could even go through the underarm. There were several doctors recommended, conveniently located in the area. Stephie said if I used her doctor, she'd get a discount on her next procedure. I wondered what procedure a tall, thin 20-year-old could possibly be contemplating, but I didn't ask. These girls were serious about their surgeries, and the last thing I wanted to do was question their motives.

The longer I worked there, the more the discussion became real, like a plausible option for my life. Sure, a 20-year-old theater major in Texas needs to spend money on fake boobs. Yep, makes sense. Forget that I had tuition to pay. The fact that I was already a C cup didn't matter. Every shift I worked was like research. I was given business cards and invited to squeeze boobs. When asked if they felt natural, I'd nod my head and try not to act embarrassed by the fact that I was virtually groping Courtney or Barb. I became convinced that having a boob job was just a pre-emptive strike against gravity. I thought it might help me land acting roles. I would get better tips. Maybe I'd have a chance at the calendar. My brain spun with the possibilities.

Then came the Fourth of July, possibly the biggest holiday in the Lone Star State. I was scheduled to work the evening shift since I was a new girl, but I got called in early. Apparently, several girls didn't show up so they could go party. I ended up working a double shift with a huge section. My usual section consisted of about four or five tables. This one had 13, including a table shaped like Texas that could've sat the Texas Rangers.

About seven hours into the monster-shift, I was really in the weeds. I felt terrible. I wanted all of my tables to be happy, but I couldn't seem to get it together. My feet burned and my back throbbed. I was pulled aside by my manager. I thought I was in trouble. Table 8 had been waiting for over half an hour while they attempted to change out the Bud Light taps, and at least three other tables were waiting for checks. I was sure my career as a Hooters girl had come to an abrupt halt.

My manager looked pissed. Ready to explode. It was the first time I'd seen her when she wasn't composed and bubbly. We stood in the hallway between the walk-in fridge and the restaurant. Behind her I could see busboys running and people looking around impatiently. The ground was littered with napkins, wing sauce and the occasional stray curly fry. The place was a mess. My section looked like the wreckage after a tornado.

I took a deep breath.

She folded her arms across her perfect rack. As always, I was struck by how flawless she looked. The shiny, long blond hair swung behind her, the pink lipstick glistened and the porn-star eye makeup crinkled as she glared at me. Then she told me that my own makeup was wearing off. "A Hooters girl always has her face on. Now, get in the bathroom and fix yourself," she said, tossing her hair.

"But I don't have time. Tables are waiting for food." Now the firing would come.

"People don't come to Hooters for the food, honey pie. Now, go make yourself pretty. And remember to keep your makeup pristine. This is your first warning."

My first warning? Could they fire me for not enough blush? Was that even legal? There was so much I wanted to say to my Barbie-like manager. No matter what I did to my appearance, I never measured up. But my tables were waiting. I pushed the anger down, slapped on some lipstick and finished my shift.

Over the next few days, that conversation kept nagging at me. I replayed it in my head over and over. I couldn't believe that a little lipstick was actually more important to the company than good service. I wasn't so ignorant as to imagine that people came to Hooters for the food. I knew that the customers were there to gawk at the waitresses. And I understood the need to represent the company and to look your best at all times. But for the first time since I'd started working there, I was struck by how superficial my job was.

And there it was. It was a job. A part-time job. Not a career or a club or anything else. Yes, the money was great, but why should I consider permanently altering my appearance to fit in at a college job? Had I become as empty and vapid as the girls I secretly made fun of?

I worked at Hooters for a couple of months longer. I think I finally realized that I was never going to fit in there and I was sick of trying. It took me years to get over the fake tanning and the acrylic nail addiction, but I did it. I'm off the stuff for good. Oh, and I still have my own breasts. No, you can't feel them. You'll have to take my word for it.

Up Front

by
Terri Elders

Even though Mama always warned me to be careful what I wished for, I had no doubt I wanted a padded bra for Christmas. I wished for one when I blew out the candles on my 12th birthday and when I split the Thanksgiving wishbone with my sister. Once I even sneaked outside late at night to search for a falling star to wish upon.

I had skipped a grade, so felt dwarfed by the other girls in seventh grade who wore bras, whether they needed them or not. I'd seen a few stuffing Kleenex in their bras in the girls' restroom, but in the gym showers I recognized that most of the girls already had no need for such artifice. I did.

I'd heard of training bras, but thought that sounded like something for wannabe 10-year-olds, just one step up from an undershirt. I longed for the real article, a lacy 32AA with some slight padding to give me the illusion of curves. My older sister, Patti, had bras, and I wanted one, too.

Actually, *wanted* might be too mild a word to describe how incredibly desperate I was to be able to look down and see something other than my slightly knobby knees. I pined, I yearned, and I hankered and hungered. Sometimes at night I'd pat a hand across my concave chest as I called for divine intervention. *Not too big,* I'd whisper, *but just a little something to distinguish me from my little brother.*

At first my parents had scoffed at my gift request.

"Christmas is a time for games, for things you really need. Coats, for example. Not for underwear," Mama said.

"A bra? That's silly," Daddy said.

Patti agreed that she, for one, needed a new coat, a pea jacket just like the other girls were sporting that winter.

But I whined and wheedled, moaned and groaned, until finally Mama sighed, shook her head and said, "We'll think about it." Daddy grumbled, but I knew I had won. When Mama thought about something, it got well-thought, and I knew she wanted me to be happy. And to look nice. She'd always reminded me to wear clean shorts when I went to play tennis, and to wash my hair when I came home from the playground pool.

On Christmas morning Patti opened her present first, the biggest box under the tree. She pulled out a navy blue pea jacket and squealed with delight. She threw it on and vamped around the living room as if she were parading down a catwalk. I had to admit she looked chic indeed in the stylish broad-lapelled coat with its slash pockets and big wooden buttons.

My old red wool jacket will get me through another winter, I told myself, even though I had noticed it was getting snug across the shoulders. I reached for my package, much smaller, but equally gaily wrapped. I opened the box and spied, nestled among the tissue, not one, but *two* delicate brassieres!

My father and brother looked the other way when I pulled them from the box, but Mama and Patti smiled. I scampered into the bedroom to try one on and nearly cried for joy when I saw myself in the mirror. I had a bosom, at long, long last. For the next few hours I preened, pretending not to notice my brother's knowing smirks.

Later that day we prepared to drive to Grandma's for Christmas dinner. Since the temperature in late December had dipped into the low 40s—cold for Southern California—I threw on my old red jacket. But when I started to button it up, I realized I had a problem. No matter how hard I tugged, the buttons wouldn't slip into the buttonholes; they fell about half an inch too short. The culprit was my Christmas bra. The padding added just enough girth to my front to render the coat unbuttonable. And red wool did not fall into the category of a stretch fabric.

I had a choice. Either remove the bra or go to Grandma's coatless. I chose the latter, yanking the Army blanket from my bed and wrapping it around my shoulders. Nobody said anything when we piled into the back seat, but I couldn't help but notice how pretty and warm Patti looked in her new coat.

"She's really growing up," Grandma said, marveling at my enhanced figure, even though she'd seen me the week before and must have known I couldn't have developed that much that fast. Grandpa just did a silent double take.

When school started after winter break, I knew I'd have to put the bras aside until the weather got warmer. I couldn't substitute my Army blanket on the long hike to the bus, so I would have to button my jacket against the chill. I thought about tucking a bra into my zippered notebook and sneaking into the restroom before class, but remembered how embarrassed those girls had looked when I saw them with the Kleenex. I decided against making myself a laughingstock. The bras would wait for their school debut.

By spring I had grown 2 inches and gained 10 pounds. On the first day balmy enough to head for the bus without my old jacket, I eagerly pulled one of the bras from the drawer where they had languished all winter. *So pretty*, I thought, as I stuck my arms through the straps and reached behind to fasten the hooks.

I couldn't get it hooked. I took it off and stared at it in disbelief. The 32AA was now too small. Then my eye fell on something else, something softly rounded.

"Be careful what you wish for," Mama had said. Thank heavens my birthday was coming up soon. I knew exactly what to wish for. A new jacket in a larger size. Because it was suddenly clear that Mama and I would have to go to the store for underwear before then. Probably right away!

Terri (left) and older sister Patti

Battle-Dressed Breasts

by

Laurel McHargue

Although Army Battle Dress Uniform (BDU) designers knew what they were doing when they were tasked to create the perfect camouflage for soldiers, they probably could not have anticipated an unlikely scenario that unfolded at a rest area on the other side of the world. This odd occurrence nearly became the grounds for an international incident.

My company was part of a Team Spirit exercise. It was 1989. Our journey from Fort Ord, California to Pusan, (now Busan) South Korea was exhausting. As Commander of the 301st Transportation Company, I was responsible for getting half my company and its equipment deployed for our three-month tour of support for the annual exercise. Bleary-eyed and feeling fairly grungy once we disembarked and regrouped in Pusan, we still had a long journey waiting as we boarded multiple buses which would carry us much further north to our destination in Osan.

I cannot remember how long we were cooped up on the buses before we hit the first rest stop, but the need to pee was ferocious, and I led the way to the ladies room with two of my female soldiers.

We had barely made it inside the spacious bathroom when the attack began. The sudden cacophony of high-pitched, disgruntled voices startled us all, yet we were unprepared for the physical assault that ensued. Tiny little hands—attached to tiny little old-as-dust Korean women—tugged and pulled at our sleeves in an attempt to drag us out of the bathroom! The situation was disturbing, especially since by then, my eyes were about to turn yellow. There was no way I was leaving without relieving, and I knew that my soldiers were hurting as well.

It took a moment before it dawned on me that these little old ladies—barely chest high to me—probably thought that we were in the wrong restroom. After all, we were covered cap to boots in military field attire. *An easy fix,* I thought, removing my cap and attempting to talk with my adorable captor. But no such luck. With barely a glance at my face—which by this time was likely as greasy and colorless as my conservatively cropped hair—our elderly assailants continued their struggle to drag us to the door, and my soldiers continued to look to me with desperation in their eyes.

In a sudden moment of clarity, I knew what to do. It was time to bring out the big guns, so to speak. Not that I couldn't have overpowered my wizened little warrior and removed myself from her grasp, but I didn't want to be rude. I was, after all, an ambassador of sorts, and both the situation and the noise decibels had already escalated to a point that made me uncomfortable—on multiple levels. No, I knew what to do.

With one fancy-foot maneuver, I positioned myself between my malcontent and the doorway, disengaging my sleeve ever so gently from her grasp, and with my two hands now freed, I clasped them to my own camouflage-covered breasts and—as much as I could under those bulky, buttoned-down pockets—shook them in her face (which, as I have heretofore mentioned, was chest high to me).

If only I had had a third hand holding a camera at that abrupt moment of comprehension! The eyebrows on that scrunched-up, ancient face were suddenly lost in her hairline as this new reality dawned on her. The noise which had moments before sounded like a Girls-Gone-Wild bar brawl now became, although no less loud, uproarious laughter. I had no idea what conversation passed between these little old ladies, but suddenly they were like children in a toy store, and we were the toys. The little hands that at first held us captive now boldly and unapologetically explored the G.I. Janes in their midst, turning us round and round while patting our not-so-camouflaged-anymore lady lumps.

With the crisis thwarted, my soldiers and I had yet to accomplish our mission, so with universal cross-legged-belly-holding-gotta-pee sign language, we were finally released to relieve ourselves. A third hand would have come in handy for this endeavor, too, as the balance required to straddle the hole on the floor of the bathroom stall while ensuring that the ass of your BDU pants is pulled forward and away from the target zone would have made any trained gymnast proud.

Our still giggling new friends waited for the three of us

to complete our task, and resumed feeling us up as we made our way—this time, happily—to the door. Upon stepping back into the sunlight together, we were startled once more to see the concerned crowd that had gathered outside during the course of our international incident. In no time, however, the laughter and chatter of those boisterous little women brought smiles to the throng, and we boarded our bus with a story that has never failed to entertain.

Laurel sporting her classy BDUs while in Korea.

Laurel's mom, Patricia Bernier, visiting her daughter in Korea.

Almost Barely Complete

by

Valerie Benko

My older sister fetched a shirt from her closet and tossed it my way.

"My boobs aren't big enough to hold this up," she remarked.

I caught the shirt and proudly held it up against me. *Yep, I shouldn't have any problem making it fit,* I thought to myself.

A long time ago, I had a much smaller chest than my sister. I remember trying on clothes in the same fitting room as her and being filled with envy as I admired her B cups, which seemed huge compared to my flat chest. Now I've surpassed her with a C.

She sized me up before remarking, "You don't want those any bigger, do you?" It wasn't really a question, but more of a statement, one that I was sure was laced with longing. I was content with a respectable C, but it was a long journey in growing them.

Boobs weren't important until high school. I had been a tomboy with a ponytail and dirty knees, spending my free time scaling chain-linked fences, playing softball and trying not to fall out of trees.

In sixth grade, the boys would sneak up behind unsuspecting girls and snap their bras, giggling as the girls shrieked. I was relieved I didn't even own one and was left out of these games. But that summer, my older sister decided I needed to wear one and to start shaving, as well. Thus, I was slowly being introduced to one of womanhood's rites of passage.

When I started high school, I was still wearing a training bra or something akin to one. The flimsy white piece of material didn't have cups—since I had nothing to put in them—and I could ball the whole thing up in my hand. Plus, I'm pretty sure there wasn't even a size on the tag!

I started noticing breasts everywhere. All of my friends had them. They wore cup sizes I could only dream about and they shopped at exclusive bra boutiques like Victoria's Secret and Frederick's of Hollywood. New words such as *padded* and *underwire* were added to my vocabulary.

Boob envy set in. I longed for my mosquito bites to grow into something voluptuous. I had ulterior motives for wanting them. It wasn't to fill out my shirts or to turn heads while sporting a hot bikini or to complain about them bouncing in gym class like the other girls did. It was for one reason and one reason only—BOYS!

Straight A's in high school came easy, landing me on the honor roll time after time. I even graduated with honors in my pursuit of academic excellence. The only thing I didn't want straight A's in was my bra size. Boys didn't like brains. They liked breasts. And I didn't have any.

Being flat-chested made the boyfriend situation interesting. I specifically remember one of them fumbling around my upper half during a makeout session, trying to find my twins. The problem was that I was lying on my back, which made them disappear altogether!

As college selection came around, I was overjoyed to discover that the girls had grown into a full A cup. I was almost there. And college proved to be no different than high school. Boobs were everywhere. There were Dangs and Double Dangs. One girl even told me she wore an E. *What the heck is that?* I thought. To me, E meant empty, but not in Bosomland. Here, E meant "Everything is overflowing" or "Emergency breast reduction."

When bar hopping, my bigger-breasted friends drew obvious stares from guys. The only stares I got were when I tripped over a bar stool, spilling my Sex-on-the-Beach drink all over the place.

Somewhat desperate to look like I had boobs, I tried padded bras, water bras and gel bras, but I hated them all. They were heavy and uncomfortable and felt as fake as they were. I just wanted to be natural. One day, after showering, I noticed roundness to my breasts that had never been there before. My bras were fitting tighter and I assumed they had shrunk. In my quest to find a new bra, I happily discovered that I was a B. Barely there, like the brand of my bra.

I knew I was getting closer to boob perfection when a guy came up to me in a bar where they were advertising a wet T-shirt contest and suggested I enter. I laughed off the request, telling him I wouldn't even qualify. He remarked that he would have voted for me, before he and his bottle of beer disappeared into the crowd. I stood alone waiting for my friends to return and felt a slight twinge of happiness. B's were noticeable!

On college graduation day, I proudly walked my B's across the stage and accepted my diploma. Life was just beginning for me and the girls.

I was satisfied with a B cup. I loved how my body looked in clothes and how the girls didn't disappear when I lay down. Boys were no longer a problem and one even asked me to marry him. But every now and then a C caught my eye and I wondered just what life would be like.

I was soon to find out. As I was trying on wedding dresses, I realized the dresses were a bit snug in the breast area. A smile lit my face. I was finally C-omplete.

The girls were definitely getting attention now and I started experiencing foreign discomforts such as men talking to them instead of me and the crazy way well-formed breasts bounced when I ran upstairs.

At a party at my sister's house, one of my breasts tipped a bottle of beer as I was reaching across the table. One of the men quickly grabbed it before it spilled and muttered, "Her big breast almost spilled my beer."

In that moment I knew I was legit. My boobs had arrived! I was no longer on the outside looking in. I was finally one of the girls that I had spent so much of my life envying. I looked at my sister leaning against the counter talking to one of her guests. Maybe someday she, too, will be almost barely complete.

Cream or Sugar?

by
Dianna Graveman

My mother was a very proper lady. She was always dressed impeccably, and her manners were above reproach. Not a single plunging neckline lurked among the many finely-woven sweaters and blouses hanging in her closet.

According to my mother, women did not have periods. Instead, they had "that time of the month" or their "monthly visitor." And they did not get pregnant; they became "that way." ("Did you hear Molly is that way? She missed her monthly visitor.")

Once, while discussing birth experiences with a family friend, I announced that an acquaintance who had previously delivered via caesarean section had just delivered her second child vaginally. I thought Mom was going to choke on her coffee. Vagina—and all of its derivatives—was a word nice girls didn't say in public.

Breasts were never talked about, either. For my mom, they existed only as an unnamed part of the general body area known as "the chest." The only time I heard her use the word "boob" was in reference to television (i.e., the "boob tube") and its stupid programming.

So when I told her I was going to breast-feed my first child, she was dismayed. Even though the breast-feeding movement had gained some speed in the mid-1980s and pediatricians were touting its benefits for both mother and baby, my mom still refused to believe breast milk could be as good for my son as formula. After all, Mom had bottle fed both my brother and me, and we had turned out just fine, hadn't we?

Grudgingly, Mom went along with my decision to breast-feed (we called it "nursing" and never once used that *other* word), but she was visibly relieved when I weaned my son and returned to work two months later. During the mid-1980s, workplaces weren't as friendly to nursing moms as they are today, and finding some place private to pump breasts or store milk was difficult. I'm ashamed to say I chose not to buck the system.

Then BABY TWO came along, and Mom almost got her wish for a bottle-fed newborn. A difficult birth and related health issues forced my baby to remain in the hospital after I'd been released. This time, however, I did buck the system and pumped like a madwoman whenever I had to be away from the hospital. I continued to nurse for many months after my baby came home.

By the time BABY THREE arrived, I thought myself quite the breast-feeding expert. I was convinced I would breast feed this time for at least a year, a fact I conveniently forgot to share with Mom each time she asked, "Isn't it time to put that baby on a bottle now?"

Round and round we went, month after month, Mom pushing, me pulling, while my baby happily suckled at my breast.

With the first two babies, I had been squeamish about nursing in public. With the third, I got brazen and nursed her everywhere. I was very discreet—blankets over the top of me on the warmest of days. Mom was less than convinced when I told her nobody could see a thing. I'd whip out that blanket, and Mom's face would go white and then red, as if I'd just whipped out my boob instead.

Then it happened—my worse-case scenario. Mom had asked me to join her for a late lunch. The restaurant was almost empty and I figured I was safe. My baby was hungry and started to cry, so out came the blanket. Mom's face did its typical color change before she set about sipping her decaf and pretending she didn't know what I was doing.

Along came the server to refill our cups. She was young and unworldly, and she obviously didn't realize what was happening under that blanket, which—at first—I thought was a good thing.

"Oh, a baby!" she squealed, once it dawned on her what was under wraps. "Let me see." She lifted a corner of the blanket before I could stop her.

My baby, suddenly distracted, stopped nursing and turned toward the voice. And my breast milk, with no little mouth to catch it, squirted across the table and onto the server's apron, depositing a few drops into the coffee carafe on its way. Whoops!

Quickly, I glanced around. The restaurant was still empty. Nobody was looking. Still, I knew I was doomed. I hung my head. Mom would never, ever forgive me for such a public display of a bodily function.

Then I heard a snicker—my mom's. Followed by a guffaw—the server's. Soon the three of us were laughing so hard that tears streaked our faces, and the server was weakly holding on to the end of our table for support.

From then on, it was Mom's and my private little joke. Every time I'd pull out the blanket and begin to nurse, Mom would giggle and whisper to me from behind her hand: "Be careful, now, or you might get a little extra cream in your coffee."

The Ice Bra Cometh

by
Monica Giglio

"Only you, Monica. This stuff only happens to you."

In the past decade as a single mother of three, I'd heard that declaration more times than I could count. I don't ask for drama to come into my life, but it somehow finds me. Freaky stuff happens, like when the washing machine repairman mortified my teenage daughter by saying, "Aha! This is the culprit!" while pulling her rainbow-colored thong out of the pump. Or when my lingerie got stuck on a baffle in the dryer and caused a small house fire. But like my mother before me, when I fall down, I get up quickly, and when I get embarrassed, I laugh!

My 11-year-old daughter, Sarah, had been playing the same practical joke on me for three months. She'd hide my water bras in the freezer, and then sneak them—completely frozen—into my drawer just before I'd get dressed. I'd bought these bras not because they were extra plump, but because I could get three for less than $20. And they came in the most important bra colors: white, tan and black! It wasn't until I got home that I realized they were liquid-filled. It's not like I thought I needed extra padding, extra support or extra anything. OK, maybe underwire support, considering I have given birth to, and nursed, three children. But mostly I just couldn't resist a bargain.

One summer day when I was particularly parched, I reached into our freezer for ice cubes and found nothing in the ice bin. On closer inspection, I saw a batch of ice about to be expelled from the ice maker, but appeared to have stopped mid-motion, half way through the act. Many of the cubes had morphed into a solid ice mass, now frozen into the ice maker. It dawned on me that I had not heard the grind of ice making for several days, since before my daughters left for a weekend with their dad.

I gave the ice behemoth a tug, a tap, a slap and a few curse words, but it didn't budge. I turned the ice maker off and back on. The motor would start to churn and the auger, which rotated the ice cubes from the tray, would jiggle for a second then immediately stop. Something was preventing it from completing the last segment of a full rotation to dump the ice and produce the next batch.

Investigating further, I blindly reached up into the ice-making mechanism and feeling along the sharp metal edges of the cube separators, I prayed that the contraption wouldn't spontaneously start turning! Not one to shrink in fear, I stuck my head in the freezer for a better look.

Pressing my cheek against the ceiling of the freezer and peering sideways into the ice maker, I could see a larger frozen accumulation caught in the auger. *What was it? Another ice mass?* I wondered to myself.

Not wanting to pay for my repairman to come out and rescue me, I decided to fix this problem myself. Instead of defrosting the entire freezer, I used my blow dryer as a torch. Taking aim at the auger, I melted as much of the ice as possible in an effort to free the machine. I was making progress, but the melting ice dripped in a steady stream all over the frozen vegetables and strip steaks. "No problem. Don't sweat the small stuff. I'll clean the water up later," I mumbled to no one in particular.

A few minutes later, my blow-dryer torch must have activated an automatic sensor to produce more ice! Suddenly, the water supply kicked on and water began gushing into, and out of, the freezer at a rate of what seemed to be gallons per minute! It was pouring all over the freezer's bottom, cascading down the front of the fridge, and streaming onto the kitchen floor! We lived on the top floor of a condo and my biggest fear at that instant was the water leaking into the neighbor's condo below me! The last thing I wanted was that self-important old fart interrogating me because she would more than likely file a claim with the homeowner's association and they, in turn, would get all up into my business.

I had to act quickly. Running to the laundry room, I turned off the water supply and grabbed towels from the dryer to sop up the kitchen floor. Once I got the semi-flood under control, I peered back inside the freezer. Before me was the guilty party, still somewhat encased in ice—my favorite water bra! Sarah had been at it again!

Try as I might, the bra would not come free—it was tangled

around and frozen into the auger. I had to think of a solution quick if there was any hope of extricating it without the embarrassment of calling my repairman yet again. *A thong in the washing machine pump, lingerie fire in the dryer and now a bra in the freezer? Geez, lady,* I imagined him saying to me, *You have another wild, drunken, crazy party or what?* No, I couldn't tell him about this and maintain my good reputation. So with renewed fervor, I got back to work.

When I had melted all the ice, I still could not extricate the bra. I grabbed the undergarment with two hands, put one foot against the fridge, and yanked hard! Nothing. I began to think I'd have to call for the Jaws of Life! My only option was to cut the bra into pieces. I had no idea what the gel-like substance in the bra's undercup contained and feared contaminating my ice supply if I cut into it and the mystery goop spilled out and into the freezer. *Will my family be poisoned? Is it worth that risk?* Yes, these are the freaky thoughts you have when there's a water bra stuck in your freezer.

With pliers, snips, wire-cutters and lots of elbow grease, I attacked the remains of my white bra. Determined, I carefully snipped away until all that was left was the underwire and a few shreds of fabric. But yet, I still could not yank it completely free. Then after what seemed like hours of hard labor, a wonderful thing happened. The heavens opened, the white lights flooded into my kitchen and a hallelujah chorus played melodiously—the auger turned on its own. There were no ice cubes to dump. No ice had been produced in days. The auger simply turned, and when it did, the remains of my bra were expelled from its clutches and dropped into the ice bin with a thud and a clank! It really was as simple and as wonderful and as beautiful as that.

Even though I am now minus one water bra, at least I had ice cold beverages for the remainder of the summer. The previously frozen and now shredded remains of my bra have been preserved in our family history and have been given an honored place in our scrapbook/photo album along with other memories of that summer, the summer when the ice bra cometh . . . undone.

Monica on a mission!

CHAPTER FOUR

Hear Me Roar

We are women,
so get the hell out of our way!

Harley and the Harridan

by
Janet Hall Svisdahl

"Why am I blue? Look at me and tell me!" I demanded.

"You don't look blue, just kind of red."

I leapt off the back of the Harley Davidson and pulled off my helmet, glancing in the small side mirror at my windblown, sun-bleached hair.

"I'm blue because since I've been sitting on the back of this Harley," I said, exasperated. "I've been doing a lot of thinking." As I talked, Randy smeared a generous helping of sunscreen over my sunburned face.

"Uh huh," he responded helpfully, trying not to sound impatient, only to let me know he was listening.

The two brothers had an agenda. We women had to keep up. "Just because I'm feeling chunky and unshaved, with hair sprouting nose to toes, there is no need for me to have an attitude," I muttered darkly, wishing with all my heart I could have had a bath that morning. But there was that agenda—there'd been no time.

"I do have a problem," I confessed, sunscreen making its way into the corner of my mouth.

"Yes," Randy said bluntly, "You do have a problem. You look fine."

Fine? I thought, feeling insulted. *What woman wanted to look fine?* In reality, my problem had nothing to do with feeling chunky and unshaved, or the fact I had had no time to prettify myself. It had to do with the fact that we had just passed through a border town where young, physical perfection reigned supreme. Up to that point, I had been kind of enjoying this motorcycle trip with Randy, his brother Wiley, and Diana, Wiley's girlfriend. And I was also enjoying the great change of life I was going through. But now, seeing youthful perfection everywhere I looked, all I could think about was how fast I was aging. Those cute twenty-somethings in the border town, with their perfect skin and perfect hair and perfect figures, wearing perfect short shorts and perfect bikinis, dismally reminded me of how quickly my body was altering.

I couldn't get over it. Really, I couldn't. It was a sad, vain fact. I sighed. "A mere moment ago I was thinking I was pretty hot!" I muttered pitifully while Randy put the sunscreen away in his leather pocket, ". . . when I clean up." With a helpful nod from my guy to show he was listening, I proceeded unsurely, "But these beauties, walking by in their tight skin, with legs the likes of which I'll never see again, tell me otherwise. I'm *not* hot!"

"Uh huh," Randy answered, now absent-mindedly applying lip balm to my chapped, sun-baked lips, probably wishing he was in the restaurant quaffing down a cold beer with Wiley.

"You're not blue, honey. You're having a hot flash," he said evenly, "having endured hours of 104-degree heat on the back of the bike. I think you need something cold to drink."

"I am too blue!" I yelled into his deaf ear, exasperated. "I know I'll never be young and hot again!"

"It doesn't bother me," Randy said, with such stunning ignorant unconcern that it left me speechless. I gaped at him with utter incomprehension, licking my cracked lips. *It doesn't bother him?* Randy looked at his watch. *The damn agenda again.* We were supposed to make Oregon by late afternoon. *Of all the unfeeling . . .* I ran dusty fingers through my wind-tangled hair, glaring at Randy's face devoid of empathy for the female need for adulation, blissfully ignorant of a woman's need to be her man's young hot babe forever. My own face, streaked and disfigured with road dirt and blobs of sunscreen, needed clean kisses and admiring smiles, needed . . . I gripped my helmet so as not to whack Randy on the side of his head with it.

"Come on, Diana!" I shouted. Diana tumbled off the bike next to ours. She, too, looked a bit worse for wear. She almost ran into the restaurant where we'd decided to go for lunch, leaving the brothers to deal with parking the hogs.

Diana's top rode up a bit as she sat opposite me, exposing a jeweled stud on her flat tummy. She's turning 50 soon. I wondered if I should get a belly pierce, too. Self-consciously, I sucked in my poochy tummy and decided against it, hating the change of life that only hours ago I had so passionately embraced. I ordered beer, leaned in toward Diana, and we talked low and earnest about the merits of plastic surgery in order not to be overheard by the 12-year-old-looking waitress coming to our table with pen and pad in hand.

"Heaven help me," I said, picking up a menu. The waitress

wasn't really 12—she just looked like it. "I think I'll order the cheeseburger deluxe with fries."

Diana giggled. "Vacation is not the time to think about dieting."

"Yeah, you're right," I said, looking out the window in time to see a young thing leap on the back of her bike and take off. I remember when it had been that easy, when I had been limber and agile like her. I rubbed the back of my thigh where it had become bruised and sore through hours of painful hobbling on and off the Harley.

Randy and Wiley swaggered through the door in leather chaps and dark sunglasses, looking glorious, manly and virile. And, I had to admit, young.

Life was not fair.

Discreet talk of plastic surgery ceased.

After lunch, it was suggested we go for caffeine at a nearby cappuccino bar before heading back out for Oregon. Unfortunately, things happen when you age, when your hormones are all over the place like somebody's stray dog that refuses to stay home. And sometimes, caffeine makes those symptoms worse. But who cared at this point? I decided I was going to have a coffee anyway. The hot flash thermostat could take a hike into the stratosphere!

"Make it a double," I told the young server, leaning over the counter of the cappuccino bar, glaring with narrowed lids at the server's teeny tiny waist. Think female Clint Eastwood.

As I waited for my order, I looked around the bar. Big mistake. *Am I the only one my age in this place?* I wondered. Randy, wearing a scarf of cross bones, and red flames blazing down black leather, chaps molded to his perfect thighs, sauntered up to me lazily, a Harley cowboy with a cocky grin. Wiley looked equally divine as he strutted confidently beside him.

"Is there a conspiracy to make us look bad?" I whispered to Diana as I shook my gritty unwashed hair. "How do men do it?" I looked closer at Diana. Diana looked great. I wish I had the courage to scrub my face of dust in the restaurant bathroom like she had, but I wasn't comfortable bare faced. *Of course*, I said inwardly to console myself, *Diana did have her eyes done last year.* My thoughts went back to plastic surgery.

Randy tossed back his cappuccino.

"I attended a service not long ago and this 90-year-old preacher said it was a privilege to grow old." Randy said. He wiped his mouth with the back of his hand. "It's a gift of God to grow old," he added smugly.

I looked at his tanned unlined face lit with a happy smile and thumped down my cappuccino cup next to his. *Easy for him to say! He looks great!*

I strode out into the hot sunshine to the Harley, Randy following close behind. An elderly couple walked by, hand-in-hand. Looking content. Looking vibrant. I blinked as they smiled at me, their cheeks wreathed in wrinkles. *Why, they look young!* I thought, startled. As I blinked tear-filled eyes at the love shining from their faces—creased faces, worn faces—it hit me.

And I got it.

I slowly climbed onto the back of the Harley, ignoring my bruised thighs. I no longer felt blue! I felt golden! Hopeful! Joyful!

It is a privilege to grow old.

"A penny for your thoughts," Randy said, kissing me soundly as he climbed onto the Harley, settled in and turned over the ignition.

"You're hot," he mouthed over the roar, grinning mischievously at me over his shoulder.

"You can say that again," I replied, fanning myself with the menu I had taken from the cappuccino bar. "It must be in the high 90s out here."

"I mean—you're *hot!*" he said as he edged the Harley into the sweltering, late-afternoon traffic.

I'm hot? I smiled widely. The compliment, oh it felt *good*! Tonight, we'd be at a hotel with a swimming pool. Me? In a bathing suit? I was no longer unnerved. *I'm hot.*

My smile widened. Hot has nothing to do with an unlined face. Or tight thighs. Or menopause. Or even the weather. Hot is about joy. Hot is about living life to the fullest. Hot is about seeing love in the eyes of the one you love.

I donned my helmet and hung onto Randy for dear life as the Harley screamed down the highway in an explosion of youthful energy. And I tried not to notice the young firm things walking by.

Randy and Janet

For Better or For Worse

by
Ginger Kenchel

I have always been a bit of a risk-taker during my life. Being the quintessential Baby Boomer growing up in the 1960s and 1970s, I have always been a young spirit, free of the expectations society put on me regarding how I should think or act.

For example, my children were grown and gone from the nest when I met my future—yet much younger—husband while he was still in college. He was wonderful, charming, educated, gentle and so much fun, but he was also 20 years my junior. Ignoring our age difference, this amazing guy swept me off my feet. We fell in love and married when he graduated from college.

Yes, I guess you can call me a cougar.

Even though my new hubby kept reassuring me we were perfect for each other, there were times when I really felt the generation gap. For instance, while singing along to a song playing on the oldies radio station, I would ask him, "Remember this song?" He'd shake his head, and then remind me he wasn't born until the 1970s.

One day would prove to be the height of our generation gap. *Darn, it's coming on again*, I swore to myself. I had not told my young stallion that I, the woman-of-his-dreams, was starting to have hot flashes. Why? While peri-menopause was completely normal for a woman in her 40s, *moi*—you know, the aforementioned eternally-young-at-heart Baby Boomer—was nowhere near admitting that the change of life was just around the corner. And nowhere near asking her young husband to jump on board with her for a wild ride.

Why now? How can I stop it? I frantically asked myself. That warm feeling was coming back, from head to toe. The sweat rolled down my arm pits and my forehead. During many of my previous hot flashes, my husband had not been home, and if he was, the flashes were light ones that he hadn't noticed. But today, he was home in the living room, watching television—his favorite pastime. *Oh, no.*

Suddenly, in a matter of seconds, I went from warm to 1,000 degrees! I was so hot that I stripped off my soaked blouse just to try and cool down. Luckily, I was in the next room and still able to hide from my hubby the inferno blazing inside me. But I gained no relief sans blouse, so I peeled off the rest of my clothes. I then frantically looked for the floor fan and realized it had been moved into the living room—with my husband!

But the mother-of-all-hot-flashes had her claws in me and wasn't going to let go. *I need that fan, NOW!* With my mind and my body absolutely out of control, I streaked into the living room—in between my husband and his beloved television—yelling, "Hot! Hot! HOT!" Once I reached my angel of mercy, I rejoiced in the sudden wave of cool relief as the fan swept across my face and upper body—I was in hot-flash heaven. But when I turned around, to my surprise I found my husband standing in his birthday suit with a silly grin on his face!

"What do you think you're doing?!" I asked.

"You yelled 'hot!' and I thought you wanted me to play fireman!"

I know he was trying to be romantic, but I started laughing. He looked puzzled. I then explained I was going through the change. We went out that very day and bought a fan for every room in the house so there would never again be another confused signal.

As my husband and I approach our 14th wedding anniversary, I know we are meant to be. It is so nice to see a tinge of silver starting to show in his hair, and soon I will be hearing those words I have longed to hear for so long: "Honey, does it look like I'm thinning on top?"

For better or for worse . . . .

The
Kenchels

No Mountain Too High

by
Kathe Campbell

While the rest of America sweltered, sheets of rain, lightning and earsplitting thunder bumpers warned me to log off my computer and go to bed. My mammoth donkeys had fled to their barn, so I locked up and made rounds with humming and cheery chatter; animals like singing and upbeat sounds when Mother Nature puts on her show.

Old Thor up above crashed and rumbled as my dog and a bunch of scaredy cats dogged my footsteps like there would be no tomorrow. Let a bear wander through these parts, and my dog Corky is all macho and full of heroics, keeping us safe and sound. But let there be whizbanging cracks and streaks across our Montana skies, and he melts into a puddle of terror.

Corky is the second precious Keeshond to give his all when we needed him most, for my husband had been critically ill. While they spoke of bones and truck rides, our Dutch buddy spent months pressed close to Pop's wheelchair as gnarly old fingers stroked his head. Then one day our beloved Pops was gone, leaving Corky brooding against his master's pillow. My colloquy finally raising us both out of desolate depression, I spurred my buddy on, comforting his grief despite my own, for sharing our sorrow was healing. We had just braved a blizzardy spring in good shape and this would mark the beginning of our first summer going it alone.

Approaching 80, what's left of my urban friends are flabbergasted upon hearing I'm still running this mountain ranch all by myself and loving every minute of it. I may look a little worse for wear with only one arm, a new hip and crippling rheumatoid arthritis that has me lopsided and shrunken, but it would take six men and a boy to drag me away from the wilderness drama that daily feeds my soul.

That evening, half asleep in my big bed, I checked out TV's late night local news as the rain finally subsided, giving the roof a rest. But Corky was experiencing something brand new in his repertoire of senses while leering at me through panicky, black, wide-open lenses. Experts tell of wild and tame animal premonitions often, and my pup was riding out such a forewarning. Then it came, indiscernibly at first until we were shaking, rattling and rolling, reminding me of tremors I experienced on the West Coast when I was just a kid. Though both our hearts were thumping like trip hammers, I kept patting my pup, telling him all was well.

Something fell upstairs in the loft and two ceramic ducks perched atop my armoire flew down, landing safely on the carpet, along with a basket of pine cones. The kitties had scrambled under the bed, and Corky looked as though he had accepted his demise as he lay horror-stricken, ogling my every move. Finally, the TV news team announced that southwest Montana was in the midst of an earthquake, as my dog and I continued shaking. Well, duh!

After what seemed forever, the quake subsided. It had registered a moderate 5.7 for a good 20 minutes, almost 50 years after the devastating 7.2 Yellowstone disaster. This time my own mountain was to lay a mere 13 miles from the 12-mile-deep epicenter according to seismometer readings at our local School of Mines, Montana Tech.

I jumped from my bed to check out uncertain surroundings, especially the 100-year-old Douglas firs that surrounded us. The wagon-wheel chandelier in the dining room was still swaying and a wooden donkey on a shelf lost an ear as it met with the kitchen sink. After lesser aftershocks, all became still as welcomed sleep enfolded us, the late night TV comics droning on until first light.

I'm learning to be an invincible big girl now, despite years of dependence on strong men. I am woman and you can hear me roar when I darn well feel like it, for I might be momentarily rattled by mice and movable mountains, but by very little in between.

Backing Up

by
Caroleah Johnson

Women get a bad rap about their driving skills way too often. I know many women who are great drivers; one is even a race car driver. And I'm a good driver. Most of the time, anyway. Just don't ask me to back up a trailer. Perhaps that's why, one day as I set out to pick up piles of pine needles I had raked, my husband left me with very explicit instructions on where and how to drive his quad and trailer.

I could see a bit of hesitation in his eyes as he handed me the keys, warning me to keep on the dirt road and stay off the steep hills. Even though we live in very hilly terrain, I wasn't going to go four-wheeling through rocks and mud where I could get stuck. I was simply going to drive around and pick up 25 years' worth of pine needles that I had spent the previous month raking into huge piles. *How hard could that be?* I said to myself. I assured him I was fine, I knew what I was doing and he could go on to work. He had no need to worry about me. Hadn't he taught me how to back the boat trailer down the launch ramp a few years earlier? And besides, I wasn't planning to back up the quad and trailer.

I threw the pitchfork in the trailer, hopped on the quad and engaged the transmission. I putted around from pile to pile, stopping and loading huge piles of pine needles into the trailer then carting them off to a clearing where we could burn them during the rainy season. *There's nothing to it. Drive, stop, shovel, unload, drive some more.*

After several hours, I had worked my way around most of our property. With only a few piles left to load, I was at the point where I either had to back up the rig and change my direction to get to the errant piles or take the rig up the forbidden hillside. I like to be a compliant wife in most situations, and since my husband had specifically told me to keep the quad off that hill, backing up seemed to be the best option. Except that every time I tried to back up, I jackknifed the trailer.

What was it he taught me about backing up the boat trailer? Turn the wheel in the direction I wanted to go? Or was it the other way around? I tried it several times one way first then the other, but each time the results were the same. I was getting nowhere. *Well, there's more than one way to get from point A to point B; if I can't back up and I can't go up the hill, I need to find an alternate route.* Eyeing the space between the long posts that held up our back deck, I figured I had just enough room to inch my way forward between them and thus solve my dilemma.

I applied a little gas and moved forward. *So far, so good.*

The front of the quad just cleared the posts and as I started to accelerate, I heard a loud crack. I turned around to see I hadn't accounted for the back of the quad being wider than the front. *Not such a good idea after all.* How was I going to explain the cracked deck post? And how was I going to exit when I couldn't back up the trailer?

I may be a woman, but I am not a woman who easily admits defeat. There was no way I was going to let my husband come home and find the quad stuck between the deck posts, along with a significant crack in one of those posts, just because I couldn't master the art of backing up. *No problem. I'll just manually push the trailer out of the way, back up the quad, rehitch the trailer, and no one will be the wiser.* I unhitched the trailer and picked up the tongue. I gave the trailer a push. It didn't budge. I pushed again. Still nothing. Looking down, I saw one tire resting in a shallow pit. I summoned all the strength I could and pushed harder. Again. And again. Suddenly bad turned to worse as the tire popped out of the pit with such momentum that the trailer went careening down the hill. All I could do was chase after it like a crazy woman. It came to rest sideways at the base of a tree near the bottom of the hill.

I stopped to catch my breath, looked around to make sure no one witnessed this profoundly bizarre sequence of events, and then broke into hilarious laughter. I probably couldn't have staged something this funny for one of those home video shows if I had tried. But now the challenge was get the quad aligned to the trailer, rehitch it and park the rig, without any more incidents. *This is all the excitement I need for one day!* I sighed.

When my husband came home from work, he commented

on how nice the grounds looked with all the pine needles picked up. "Did you have any problems maneuvering the trailer behind the quad?"

Acting almost offended, I shrugged and said, "Problems? Of course not. You ask that like you think I'm a woman driver."

I'm not one to keep secrets from my husband, but I have learned there is an art to knowing when and how to dispense information. Someday, when the time seems right, I'll tell him how that crack appeared in the deck post. But for now, it can remain a mystery. Just like the little dent in the side of the trailer that matches the divot in the tree. After all, discretion is an important part of being a woman. And the skill of timing is every bit as important as the skill of backing up.

Life's a Classroom

by
Elsilee Patterson

Running errands is definitely not my favorite thing in the world to do, but they had to be done, even if I didn't feel like it. I had put off those deeds far too long, so long, in fact, that the margins in my to-do list were piling up to the point of the notations being indecipherable! Thus, I conquered my list one day, running those blankety-blank errands until I had accomplished all of my needed stops.

I am a responsible driver and enjoy being behind the wheel without those pesky errand interruptions. So now, my reward was looking forward to a bouncy greeting from my lovable pooch and the happy realization that I would beat the inevitable late afternoon onslaught of infamous Southern California commuter traffic.

A contented sigh escaped my lips as I saw the freeway sign announcing my exit was next. *Finally!* I thought to myself.

Checking my rear view and side mirrors, I began merging to the right to take my welcomed exit. Suddenly, I heard a loud and continuous honking of a car's horn alerting me to the presence of a vehicle in my blind spot. I swerved back into my lane just in time to avoid a collision. The car I had almost hit was now visible in my right-side mirror. Still needing to exit, I used my turn signal this time and the offended driver let me into the required lane—flashing his middle finger at me, no less—so I could get off the freeway

Shaken over the near miss, I had to pull over—I needed to collect my thoughts because I realized I could have caused that collision. Having lost both my parents instantly when a drunk driver ran a red light, and one of my former kindergarten students to a freak accident as well, I definitely had to calm down before I could continue home.

I enjoy life, and my sense of humor definitely helps this seasoned senior—with permanent handicapped license plates—deal with the physical and emotional road bumps of life. Added to my official medical diagnosis of diabetes, arthritis, depression and sleep apnea are equally debilitating self-concerns of "persona-pity-itis," "dance-and-sing-no-mournea," "cannot-get-out-of-the-bathtub-itus" and "senior-months" instead of "senior-moments," to name just a few! Plus, having been a K-1 teacher for 35 years, I miss the classroom and the students, but not the politics of teaching to the test instead of teaching the children.

Easing my car to a safe place on the ramp's shoulder, I put it in park and took a long, deep breath, exhaling slowly. Keeping my wits about me was hard, considering all of my medical issues and life, in general, which proved challenging enough.

NYMB . . . On Being a Woman

Adding a freeway fender-bender to the mix would be the straw that broke the camel's back.

I started to recline my seat ever so slightly when I heard a loud screeching sound; the driver of the car I had nearly hit pulled in behind me and blocked any avenue of escape! The driver got out of his car and loudly slammed the door shut. He headed toward me quickly with an angry look on his face that said, "Lady—you're dead!"

Please, God, help! I've no clue what to do! I pleaded silently so this enraged man would not detect how absolutely frightened I was. When he pressed his nose virtually against my driver's-side window, it struck me that his contorted face looked like a 6-year-old, ready to throw a fit. Just as he opened his mouth to spew out words I most assuredly did not want to hear, I opened my window just a smidgen. Putting on my best kindergarten-teacher smile, I said, "Thank you so much! You were in my blind spot and if you hadn't honked your horn, we would have had a collision. I've had a frustratingly long day and I need an accident right now like I need a hole in my head! I just want to get home and relax! Thank you so much for being an alert and vigilant driver. I'm exceedingly grateful!"

As the enraged man listened to my profuse praise, I delighted in watching his facial expressions. They quickly progressed from unchecked anger through huffiness, shock, confusion, puzzlement, disbelief and, finally, questioning. It was then I realized how unaccustomed he must have been to receiving positive comments. If his aggressive behavior to me was an indication of his usual approach to others, any kind of praise was probably scarce and unexpected in his life.

With his aggression now replaced by a quizzical look, he turned and walked away with a macho swagger, casually saying over his shoulder, "Well, you're welcome!"

Driving home, an anxious rush of adrenaline over this near accident and run-in was replaced by a wave of fatigue. I was pleased my women's intuition had kicked in, but realized that the change I witnessed in this fellow was probably temporary. More than likely, he may well flash the peace-sign-minus-one in the future to another driver, but probably not today!

The Pinup Girl

by

Joyce Newman Scott

My husband reminded me to go grocery shopping. I hate shopping for food and agree to it only because it's my job and obligation as a good wife, although I never read it in the marriage vows. Do they really say to love, honor and do the food shopping?

But every week since I've started school at Florida International University, a late-in-life decision I admit, the conversation goes like this: "Honey, don't you think it's time to get plastic bags, ice cream—the chunky kind—and dog food? Oh yeah, bread, ham, cheese and steaks . . . "

Well, you get the idea.

On Friday of last week, I found myself at the grocery store sprinting down the dairy aisle. I felt a cart close behind me, but I didn't stop to turn around. My focus was to get in and get out as quickly as possible. I have been known to throw a container discus-style from 50 feet into my food cart—call me

Michael Jordan. (Hint: cold cuts fly especially well, and they don't splatter when they hit—or when you miss.)

I moved on to the meat section and felt the rush of adrenaline; I was almost done! Reaching for the rib-eye steaks, I heard an older female's voice next to me: "You should be a model. Someone should take a picture and send it in to one of those magazines. I mean, everything about you—your hair, your face, your body—they all work."

Well, what could I do? If someone tells you that you look like a model, especially if you're over 50, you stop and talk with them. I wanted to kiss her, actually. I didn't think I'd looked that great when I had left the house that morning. Now she was telling me I looked glamorous.

She was about 70 years old, and she looked darn good herself. Her hair was gray but well-styled, and she had a petite body and well-shaped jaw line with high cheek bones.

I tried to sound modest. I'm not sure if it worked. What I really wanted to tell her was that I'd been a model most of my life. Not anything big-time, like Cindy Crawford, but in my 30s I'd had enough small jobs to earn a living. I was the ditzy brunette who said, "You'll love it at Levitz." But now I was older. In the last few years the economy dropped. When that happens, so do advertising campaigns. The terrorist attack on 9/11 didn't help. At 50, I'm in a non-existent category—too old to play the slice-of-life housewife and too young to sell pharmaceuticals. My next big earning market will be in my 60s, if I survive and I'm still breathing. Instead of crying in my beer, I decided to stop waiting for agents to call with job offers and registered for college courses, taking creative writing.

But what did this woman care about my modeling career? She stared at my face, not willing to let the subject go.

"No, really. You look good."

"You mean for my age," I said. I knew that's what she really meant.

"How old are you?" she asked.

"Fifty-three."

"I never would have known if you didn't tell me."

"We both look great for our ages."

I guess that was the wrong thing to say. She smiled, searching for the right words—her lips opened into a round hole—but nothing came out. Then I realized that I'd made her uncomfortable. I tried to look at the steaks in the freezer, anywhere but her eyes.

She leaned over her cart. "I've been out in the sun much of my life. All of this," she said, pointing to her face with her index finger, "is wrinkled now." I saw her eyes travel back into another world, and I waited patiently for her story. She didn't disappoint me.

"I worked for my father. We used to raise chickens. I'd go out and collect the eggs while the hens were setting. One day someone took a picture of me in a big straw hat and sent it in to a magazine. It appeared overseas."

I don't know why, but I could suddenly see how she must have looked back then: long brown hair flowing in the breeze of the summer wind, teeth glistening in the sunshine, and Betty Grable shorts that showed all of her curves. She was beautiful.

"One of my friends called and asked, 'Aida, what are you doing overseas?' I laughed and told them the picture was taken here in Miami. I'd never left. I'd never been outside of Florida. But there I was, overseas in a magazine. These boys were pinning that picture up of me over their beds at night. Can you imagine that? I was a pinup girl."

I felt a lump form in my throat. I was witnessing a great moment in time. She was talking about World War II. She had been the reason why so many of our boys, now our grandfathers, had come back home. She was their inspiration.

There are days when you have to do things you don't want to do. If you do them, sometimes there is a reward at the end— if you take the time to see it. She was mine.

Smackdown

by
Barbara Carpenter

Like most August mornings in South Central Illinois, the sun touched the whole outdoors with a golden shimmer, a promise of the white-hot heat that would follow. I slid under the steering wheel of my two-door, light blue Bonneville, cool from its shady parking spot beneath the trees that lined our driveway. I rolled down the windows and let the wind have its way with my long hair, uncut for seven years.

I felt pretty in my new blue top and narrow skirt. At 22, in love with my handsome farmer husband and the mother of a curly-haired, blue-eyed toddler, I had the world by the tail on a downhill grade! I could not have been happier, and I might have felt a bit smug about it.

Smiling, I patted the chubby little legs of my daughter who sat hip-to-hip with me. Seat belts were not yet mandatory and very few cars had them. Grandma's house was my little one's favorite destination, and she chattered non-stop all the way there. My 15-year-old sister-in-law vied for my daughter's affections, and she squealed when her aunt ran out to meet us, ready for a shopping trip to the nearby small town.

"Hi, baby." She drew my excited child into her lap. The two of them had a rapport more like sisters than aunt and niece, but then less than 14 years in age separated them. Even so, the teenager appeared a bit older than her years, always a plus at that age. Seven years her senior, I had barely left the magic teen years behind. However, becoming a mother made me feel older, as if I had suddenly attained adulthood.

We chatted and laughed as we made the rounds and ran errands, taking turns carrying the baby when she grew tired. On the way home, we pulled into the parking lot of The Chuck Wagon truck stop for lunch. Every small town in America probably had a similar place. Famous for its fried chicken, the restaurant never lacked customers.

Just as I turned off the ignition, a car pulled into the space beside us, on my driver's side. I glanced briefly out the window, and my eyes met the direct gaze of the young man in the passenger seat, no more than three feet from me. A brilliant smile filled the face of this dark-haired stranger. His eyes were not as beautiful as my husband's, my criteria for judging all blue eyes. Still, he was handsome.

"Well, hi," he said. I grinned back at him and tilted my head, not quite flirting, but almost.

"Hi," I replied. I glanced at my sister-in-law then back at the young man, whose smile grew more confident. I wanted to laugh, but I kept my secret glee hidden.

"Is the food good here?" His teeth flashed in the noonday sun. I nodded and replied that the fried chicken was excellent. "Do you eat here often?" *Had he really asked that? Really?* I thought to myself. My husband was the second boy I dated, so I hadn't been around like most girls, but even I knew he had just used a jaded pick-up line. He oozed confidence as he turned to speak to his companion in the driver's seat.

I chose that moment to open the car door and slide out, if my exit could be described as sliding. I leaned against the closed door and waited for him to turn around. The scene could not have gone better if I had written the script. I felt almost giddy, waiting for the moment.

He turned back to me. I watched his expectant smile turn to a look of near horror, followed by an embarrassed gulp. Swiftly, he averted his head. I didn't hear what he said to his friend, but over the years I have imagined various remarks he might have made: "What a shame!" "Just my luck!" "Oh, well!" "Dime a dozen!" "Someone's already been there!"

Oh, did I fail to mention that from my shoulders up I might have looked like a young, pretty, maybe even available girl, but from my chest down, my body screamed, "Young, pretty, married and seven month's pregnant!" Two months later my son was born, making our family complete.

I've thought of several things I could have said to the poor, dumb-struck would-be seducer. You know, those insane-ly witty barbs that pop into your mind days, even years, later? "Gotcha!" or "Better luck next time!" or "Sorry, Charlie!" or "I'd introduce you to my friend, but you're too old for her!"

The best come-back came to me only a few days ago—it's a

phrase I've heard used time and again in television promotions for professional wrestling matches. Thinking back at the disappointment on that young man's face, I realized I had indeed won a virtual wrestling match over his obvious intentions.

"Smackdown!"

Stirred, Not Shaken

by
Mary Eileen Williams

The experience was always so excruciating and fraught with potential psychic assault that I had postponed it as long as possible. It was only because my trip to Hawaii was swiftly approaching, thus necessitating the ungodly purchase, that I even considered attempting the agonizing activity. But I was left with little choice as our vacation neared—I needed a new swimsuit.

For sheer emotional drama alone, trying on swimsuits for me was right up there with root canals, incarceration and various forms of public humiliation. Not to say I have experience in doing all three . . . a couple, maybe, but I'll leave that up to your imagination. In truth, a swimwear purchase was no joyride even in my younger years. Now, however, being an older woman had left its all too evident markers upon my body. Facing myself, scantily clothed, in a florescent-lit dressing room replete with full-length mirror, was almost more than I could bear without consuming a few bottles of wine and going under heavy sedation beforehand.

Nonetheless, the eternal optimist in me was determined to find a great suit that would flatter my expanded figure. So, after repeating several uplifting affirmations of love and acceptance of myself in all of my matronly magnificence, I headed off to the department store. Locating the swimsuit selection, I swiftly strolled past the size-2 bikinis and headed for the mature woman's section—the one featuring dark colors, industrial-strength spandex and swim-skirts cleverly designed for that oh-so-important grand concealment.

After making my selections, I entered that chamber of horrors—aka the dressing room—to face my fate. Astonishingly, I was in for a rather pleasant surprise. *Technology does have its good side for once,* I mused to myself as I squeezed my ample hips into a swimsuit. *Not bad,* I thought after getting everything in its correct place. It became evident that major improvements in the swimsuit industry's muscle-power elastic had evolved over the years. In fact, the suit compacted my flesh with a brawny force so strong that I was pressed and squeezed within an inch of my life. It was then I realized I was unable to draw a full breath, so I couldn't save myself should I be drowning while partaking in the water offerings of the Aloha State. *Oh, well,* I sighed. But notwithstanding that one little hiccup, I was happy with the fit, so happy that I decided to venture out of my curtain-draped cubicle to brave the real test—a butt check in the three-way mirror at end of the hall.

It was then that I heard them. I parted the curtains just long enough to spot two giggling teenagers, with taut, perfect bodies, carrying in their selected suits. I quickly closed the curtains and swiftly hid myself in the dark recesses of my dressing room, thankful for a place to conceal my barely-clothed body. If I had ventured out a few seconds earlier, I would have been caught observing my backside, reflected with grandeur in that ghastly three-sided mirror, fully exposed to laughing teenage eyes and smirks of disdain.

Unaware I was there and believing they were the only two in the dressing-room area, the girls swapped tales of boyfriends, girlfriends and some real instances of teenage angst. Their feelings were openly raw as they shared stories of social slights, rebuffs and even betrayals from so-called friends. More amazingly, as they each tried on their suits, they both expressed anxieties and even pain about their bodies.

"I'm a disgusting whale!" whined one.

The other moaned in reply, "Like you should talk. I look like a fat pig with no boobs and zits on my back."

I was astounded. These girls, with their unlined skin, firm flesh and slender bodies, believed their looks to be woefully substandard and gross. They focused only on their imperceptible flaws and each seemed to suffer major distress and insecurity, while I viewed the duo as youthful perfection.

As I hid quietly in my little dressing area listening to these two, something stirred deep inside me; there was no way would I ever want to go back to being a teenager! Mercifully, I now benefited from the buffer of several decades between my present reality and my own teenage years. Remembrance of that time had, thankfully, softened into the hazy mists of recollections from long ago. The conversation I was now overhearing, however, struck me in my gut as it evoked my own teen feelings of self-consciousness and inadequacy.

How grateful I became in my eavesdropping-induced reveries to realize that I now truly enjoyed the wonders of full-fledged womanhood! My days passed pleasantly and productively, and I enjoyed my many activities. I no longer experienced hormonal moodiness nor did I obsess over every perceived slight, omission or inadvertent social snub. I had ceased my slavish need to please others and even learned to say "no" when it suited me. I was more assertive, more confident and far more self-possessed than ever before. I realized, with a rush of joy, that I really and truly liked myself! Even more so, I recognized how happy I was with my well-worn, puckered and full-figured body. This remarkable organism had experienced love, borne a child, remained healthy and served me well all these years.

I became so enthralled with my womanhood that I decided to venture out of my hiding place and strut my well-seasoned attitude in public. *I'll walk right past those poor girls with their feelings of inferiority and prance down the hallway to that three-sided mirror in all my vibrating glory!* I tittered to myself. Taking as deep a breath as possible, given the crushing force of the swimsuit, I parted the curtains and, with as much sex appeal as I could muster, I strutted to the mirror. I felt like a Bond girl shaking my stuff. The teens were just leaving and walked by me with nary a glance. There were no smirks or rolls of the eyes—they were far too engaged in their own conversation to even notice me.

When I later approached the checkout with my selected

suit, I recognized that the cashier was a woman about my age. As she removed the plastic sensor from the item, she remarked, "This one is really attractive. With your coloring, I bet it looks great on you."

"Well, thank you," I replied. "I'm really pleased."

And, as I left the store, I realized that, in every fiber of my being, I truly was.

Just Saying

Life's little moments that tickle us all . . .

Not-So-Sweet Revenge

by
Marcia Byalick

The phone rang early one Sunday evening.

"Hello, Marcia? You better sit down. You're never gonna guess who this is."

The voice was instantly familiar but like most things these days, just out of memory's grasp.

"It's been way too long," she continued, "I finally don't hate you anymore."

As far as I know, my hate fan club has only one member. I'll call her Carole. Half listening to her go on about moving, teaching, children and her divorce, my thoughts drifted back to the 1960s, to the Carole I once considered a close friend.

Two years older than me, Carole had thick, shiny black hair, beautiful black eyes and a golden tan 12 months a year, courtesy of Murray's Sun Deck, an alleyway with folding chairs on the boardwalk in Brighten Beach. We met at a local college when her warm smile and ditzy sense of humor convinced me to join her sorority. I remember the night she wore her high school prom dress at a spring break weekend just to make us laugh. She was a cashier in the campus coffee shop, and I loved paying for an English muffin and coffee, no matter what I ate. Our relationship had few conversations dealing with anything heavier than boys and bad haircuts, but it was ultimately satisfying for both of us.

In May, a year and a half into our friendship, Carole introduced me to her latest love. Bob was exotic, having graduated from an out-of-town college (the University of Buffalo!), and she swore he was "The One." They were to be pinned, she sighed, right after the summer, when she came home from working as a camp counselor out-of-state.

"Marcia, I need you to do me a favor," she said as school was ending. "I really hate leaving Bob alone all summer. What if he's lonely and meets someone else? I'd feel so much better if you'd keep an eye on him and let me know if you think I'm in trouble."

"You want me to babysit? Sure." I was working in my father's dry cleaning store that summer, and by comparison, this undercover assignment sounded positively glamorous.

I spoke to Bob twice a week and saw him often. I wrote long letters to Carole, reassuring her how much he missed her, how bored he was without her, how I wound up going to the World's Fair with him because he had two tickets and no desire to even look for a date. Every word was true. I even made the trip with Bob to visit Carole, wondering, as I watched them dance and kiss, when I, too, would be so blessed.

But when Carole came home, things weren't the same. Bob changed his mind about getting pinned. He complained she bit her nails and laughed too hard. She was devastated when they broke up.

A month later, he called and asked me out. Totally surprised, I explained I was flattered, and that although I thought he was a great guy, I could never go out with him. What kind of friend would I be if I did? He said the fact it was over between him and Carole had nothing to do with me, and that we owed our friendship a shot at exploring if it could go any further. I said "no," and then four more times over the next three months. The fifth time I said "yes." And "yes" again the next year when he asked me to marry him.

Meanwhile, Carole refused to take my phone calls or even look at me when we passed in the halls. She made sure I spent that next year as the Scarlet Woman of Bedford Avenue. So scarred was I, that a week before this particular call—although it was 24 years after the fact—I had hid behind a pillar rather than say hello to Carole's brother at Bob's 30th high school reunion.

Now she was on the phone. She chatted on a few minutes more. Then an awkward silence. I heard her take a deep breath.

"You must be wondering why I called. Well, my brother Mike mentioned Bob came alone to the Midwood reunion last Saturday. This is going to sound weird, but I figured if it's over with you guys, you wouldn't mind giving me his number. Would you?"

I glanced over at Carole's fantasy. There was Bob, wearing his shrunken, 12-year-old *Three Stooges* T-shirt that had "Just Say Mo" on the front and black sweat pants whose elastic disappeared a hundred washes ago. He lay across the bed watching his third football game of the day, washing down a soup spoon full of peanut butter with a bottle of Dr. Brown's Diet Crème Soda.

I was mortified for her, but not too mortified.

"Bob, it's for you," I said evenly, handing him the phone before leaving the room.

Bounding down the steps, I thought how it takes a woman to truly appreciate this scenario, that the wonder of being the object of an old flame's fantasy was wasted on a guy who probably wouldn't even tell his friends or revel in his coolness.

But that's OK, I love telling the story. Almost as much as I loved how I felt when Bob came out of the bedroom 15 minutes later, the glazed look in his eyes convincing me we both made the right choice.

Vajazzle My What?

by
Terri Spilman

"A Waxing Salon and More . . ."

That's the mysterious tag line from a local waxing salon that's had my friend and me scratching our heads for the past few years.

What exactly does "and More . . ." mean?

Can you buy a nice cup of Columbian coffee after you've gotten a Brazilian wax? Surely, they're not implying that after getting an excruciatingly painful back wax their clients deserve a happy ending? Nah, this is a reputable place. So the mystery continued. That is, until the other night.

(Friend): "Hey—when you get a minute, Google 'Vajazzled.'"

(Me): "Bedazzled?"

(Friend): "No! 'Va-jazzled.'"

(Me): "According to the Urban Dictionary, the definition is: 'To give the female genitals a sparkly makeover with crystals so as to enhance their appearance.' Where in the hell did you hear 'Vajazzled?'"

(Friend): "It's the answer to the 'and More' waxing salon mystery. My lady barber told me to Google it when I got home. Why don't you get that done to your muskrat?"

OK, at this point, my head is spinning and I don't know how to respond at first. For obvious reasons, I know why the lady barber probably brought up the waxing salon. Most women need an industrial vacuum to clean the bathroom after their beloved werewolf *manscapes*. She likely sharpens her clippers during a full moon.

But yet, it was gratifying to finally know the answer to the tag-line mystery. Apparently the Vajazzling process involves gluing crystals to one's va-jay-jay after the area has had a serious weed whacking.

However, WHAT THE HELL ARE PEOPLE THINKING? How did someone come up with this concept? Did a dyslexic bedazzler get Jazz Hands confused with Jazz Vag? Was it a crafter looking for another use for her Cricut heated jewels after a few too many glasses of Chardonnay? What's wrong with a blank canvas or a plain wall? Obviously, it's perfect prey for a serial bedazzler. And imagine if Eve was put on this earth with a diamond-studded apple. Might we never be here if Adam's Mr. Happy was turned into shrapnel as the result of a Vajazzle shredding?

And WHAT THE HELL IS MY FRIEND THINKING? There would have to be a crystal the size of the Hope Diamond to cover this muskrat as it is accustomed to granny panties for maximum comfort. And the glue, the itching ... the glare! The waxing salon would have to throw in a bonus pair of 98-percent UV protection sunglasses for the safety of the family. And, personally, I prefer putting a large stack of magazines on my night stand, or using the Heisman hand gesture, to send out a not-to-night-honey message instead of the Mr. Happy shredder.

The true Vajazzle test was given to my mother GemSandi, aka the QVC Diamondique Queen. After explaining the process to her, I asked her if she would partake, given her true love of jewels. Her first reaction was, "Ouch! Are you nuts?!" Then she later admitted, "Well . . . maybe if I was younger. . . "

So the mystery is finally solved. And, at least in this house, the only box that will be ridden with jewels will be my jewelry box.

The Princess and the Pimp

by
Ellen Denton

After putting my carry-on bag into the plane's over-heard compartment, I took my seat next to a black man wearing a green velvet jacket. We exchanged the usual murmured pleasantries of, "Hello, how ya doing?" But there was something in his mannerism that reminded me of pimps I'd seen on Hollywood Boulevard.

Not to stereotype any one occupational group, but years before I had worked at a restaurant at night and would curiously observe both prostitutes and pimps during the long wait for my bus home at one o'clock in the morning. The pimps did have certain characteristics in common: a challenging swagger when they walked, combined at the same time with a certain air of furtiveness, low voices and observant eyes that swept the streets with studied casualness. Those eyes would always pause for the briefest of moments if they happened to meet mine, and then swept on like a lighthouse beam.

I could never understand why a prostitute would stay involved with, let alone give her money to, a pimp, or even how the pimps would get the girls to sign on, and then, like well-trained dogs, stay.

I'm rather outgoing when it comes to communication. In the relative safety of the crowded plane, I figured nothing bad would happen to me when I turned to my seatmate and, with every bit the pleasant-traveler-making-polite small talk, asked "Are you a pimp?"

I don't recall now, so many years later, the exact words he used to answer the question, but I do recall his momentary surprise, followed by a small, sly smile, and then a flash of pride. Delivery is everything, and I know his pleased reaction was because of the way I asked the question: non-judgmentally and without the slightest trace of condemnation in my tone. Just one worldly traveler sharing sophisticated conversation with another. For him, there also seemed to be a brief, shrewd moment of considering if a new business arrangement might be at hand, but as I clearly looked more like a princess than a prostitute, he dispensed with the idea quickly.

The plane was flying from Miami to Los Angeles with a stopover about two hours into the flight, which I soon learned is where my new companion would be disembarking. I saw this as a golden opportunity to satisfy my curiosity about the strange subculture of prostitutes and pimps. I struck up a serious conversation with him, first telling him something about myself, my husband and the kind of work I did. I then told him I was fascinated with his being a pimp and how I wanted to know all about it.

Never underestimate the power of just listening. He spent the better part of the next two hours telling me not just about that, but about his entire life. On his job as a pimp, he was hesitant at first, but ended up relaying things about beating up and terrorizing the girls in his stable as well as other crimes he'd been involved in. He then went into things that happened to him growing up. He would look at me sometimes to emphasize a point, and I would nod to show I got it, but he mostly just looked off into space as he spoke, completely absorbed in the memories and in what he was saying. He would sometimes become quite animated as he recounted some dubious exploit he'd taken part in, and sometimes grow somber and thoughtful as he unearthed some long forgotten incident, which I could tell he had never before shared with anyone. His discourse was interspersed with street slang, foul language and the kind of bad grammar typical of an early school dropout.

My curiosity was satisfied. In ensuing years, I eventually let go of the small, specific details of that conversation with one astonishing exception, which to this day I recall so clearly it's as though it happened yesterday.

We had arrived at the stopover city. By that point, I felt like I'd practically known him his entire life. He was a flagrant criminal. I was a girl who looked like a princess who had a husband and a responsible job. But if you look deeply enough into the heart of another person, you'll sometimes see the most amazing things. Before he stood up to get off the plane, he turned to me, and with a genial smile and all the graciousness of a pleasant traveler politely asking a companion, "Can I give you a ride into the city?" he said, "Can I offer you a position in my organization?"

He wasn't being lewd or insulting, he didn't say it to be humorous, and he knew I would never accept his graciously proffered offer. He was simply—in his own way—being genteel. It's all in the delivery, and as strange as it may seem, as we looked comfortably into each others eyes, I could clearly see he felt it would have been rude on his part not to at least have made the offer. I of course declined it, but thanked him warmly, since I could see it was a sincere and appreciative gesture. He just, due to education, environment, the general company he kept and probably a zillion other factors, didn't know any better way to express it.

As for me, it's always been those subtle nuances of meaning that stay with me long after the words have faded away, flaring like torches along the roads of life.

Peace in Pandemonium

by
Marijo Herndon

Much of my holiday stress comes from trying to do things perfectly. Now that I'm at the age where my youthful glow is behind me, I feel I have to prove myself by being Woman of the Year. I want the perfect tree, the perfect gifts and the perfect holiday spread when I entertain. Unfortunately, I can't pull it off. The cat repeatedly knocks down the tree, the gifts are far from perfect, and one year, 20 minutes before my guests arrived, I dropped my crown roast and watched it slide across the floor until it nestled itself up against Farfel's water dish. (For any of my guests reading this, it wasn't the year you came.)

So last year to nip my stress in the bud, I thought I would treat myself to some holistic therapies. I normally address my holiday tension with a platter of Christmas cookies and a glass of milk, followed by guilt and nausea. This past year, I thought it might be time for an alternative treatment.

Feeling very brave and hip (I'm not sure if hip is still a hip word), I decided to try acupuncture. I checked around town and got the name of the best acupuncturist in my area. Upon arriving at the office, I found it to be an earthy, minimalist environment, and I began to feel tranquil just sitting in the waiting room. The doctor came out and took me into one of her treatment rooms, asked questions about my health, and then began inserting innumerous pins into my skin, starting with my head and going down to my toes. Attached to the pins was some sort of wiring that transmitted electrical impulses into my body. It was at that point that I began quoting the 23rd Psalm: "The Lord is my shepherd . . ."

She seemed very confident as she left me alone in the room with sounds of healing music playing for my enjoyment. "I'll be back in 20 minutes," she said, ignoring my chanting.

"Yeah, OK. 'Though I walk thru the valley of the shadow of death . . .'" I don't know where Dr. Needles went, but she certainly wasn't thinking about me, as she left me on her table for over an hour. She was treating a bunch of clients at the same time and apparently she had forgotten I was one of them. I would have gotten up and left, but if I tried to move in any direction, I would have impaled myself countless times with her weapons of torture.

By the time Dr. Needles came back into the room, I was in a frame of mind that could only be compared with Joanna Kearns in any Lifetime Movie Network film. I was lying there naked, tearful, shivering from the cold and terrified of this woman. I came to the conclusion after one session that this form of healing wasn't for me, especially since the fine doctor failed to remove a couple of her needles from the back of my leg, which explained the painful drive home.

My pursuit for peace and joy continued. I called my massage therapist, Sally. I had received wonderful massages in the past, so I was anticipating the same treatment. As I walked into the dimly-lit room, the soothing music, trickling sounds from the water fountain and smell of scented candles helped me relax right away. Feeling cared for and comforted, I hopped onto the table in all my glory.

"Just let the table support you, and let go of everything," Sally whispered.

Right away I could sense that something wasn't right in Sally's world. Her hands stayed on my shoulders for the majority of my hour, leaving little time for the rest of my body. I knew I had a lot of tension in my shoulders, but I had a lot of body yet to cover and my hour was almost up. With five minutes left, she massaged my back and legs with as much zeal as a dead halibut. At $70 a pop, I was disturbed at the thought of Sally having an off-day. When my service was over, I got dressed and made the mistake of voicing my concern. "Sally," I said, "you don't seem like yourself today."

A howling sound came out of her, "Oh, thank you for caring enough to ask." Wracking sobs shook Sally's body as she let go and told me all of her life's troubles. While I was hugging and consoling her, I was thinking, *I'm still going to need those Christmas cookies and perhaps something much stronger than milk to wash them down.*

I wondered if I should have stuck with the tried-and-true cookie therapy. Cookies never have a bad day; they never forget me on a table or cry on my shoulder. But they do lack that certain something. Much of my holiday stress comes from thinking that I don't measure up to the PERFECT standard. But, I guess we're not so much linked together on those days when we sparkle and shine, as we are on the days when life humbles us and sometimes even makes us laugh. Just knowing that we're all in this condition together has given me peace of mind. That's better than a cookie, any day.

Blind-Sighted

by
Pat Nelson

As a woman in my 20s with two children, my friendships revolved around other twenty-something women with babies, too. And it was during this time I learned to switch priorities from self to family.

Before children, I had been blind to the demands placed on women. But now, I no longer stayed out late. I became an early-to-bed, early-to-rise girl because I had responsibilities that I chose to face with a clear head. It was a time of growing apart from some of my childless friends. Oh, I still loved them, but they lived a lifestyle that required time and energy that I needed to devote to my children, not to myself.

Once the children started school, my interests shifted to sports, birthday parties and homework. My social life took place on the side-lines of soccer and basketball practices and games. I drove a van, so my social life also included the children and fascinating subjects like dinosaurs, Barbie dolls and armpit farts.

Time passed quickly, and my children began learning independence. I no longer drove them to games; they drove themselves. I once again participated in adult activities, watching an occasional R-rated movie or meeting friends at a bar and grill for a juicy steak (adult food!) and a glass of wine. Soon, the kids became adults. I still felt like a young woman myself, but realized that my daughter had now assumed that role, becoming a mother herself. And before I knew it, I turned 50.

At that time, a new organization—The Red Hat Society—had taken women 50 and older by storm. This occurred during a stage in my life when I had lost touch with the soccer moms and it was time to meet new friends. An organization for women aged 50 and over seemed like just the ticket for me.

Along with some of my neighborhood friends, I formed our own group—the Red Hat Tamales. At first, our group consisted of women I already knew, but soon others asked to join. We all had three important things in common: we were women, we were over 50 and we wanted to have fun.

One day, I picked up a note at my office. I almost missed the small piece of yellow paper torn from a legal pad. I glanced at the note. It read, "Call regarding Red Hat group," followed by a local phone number. I dialed the number and waited. A woman answered with a cheery hello. Her name was Maria. She explained she hadn't lived here long, and she wanted to make new friends. She thought it would be fun to join our group.

I told her about an upcoming event at a cute gift store in an old house a mile away. "Could you pick me up?" she asked.

"I don't drive."

I checked my full schedule. She didn't live far away, so I agreed. "I'll be there by 6:15," I said.

"Great," said Maria. "I'll be wearing a red jacket. I don't have a red hat yet."

I had trouble finding Maria's street, so I pulled up in front of her apartment complex 10 minutes late. She stood in the cool drizzle so common here in Washington state, holding an umbrella over her mid-length, shiny black hair. She looked sharp in the neatly-pressed red blazer. In spite of the rain and the late hour, she wore sunglasses. As she turned at the sound of my van pulling into the parking space, I saw the white cane. Maria was blind.

My thoughts flashed to my father who had spent many years with failing eyesight and, eventually, blindness. A knot of memory grabbed at my stomach.

I stepped out of my van and introduced myself, and then opened the door and guided Maria into my car. She was friendly and talkative, excited to be going out to make new friends. I was glad I had taken the time to give her a ride.

At the gift shop, I introduced Maria to other members of the Red Hat Tamales. She took out her Braille address book and recorded names and phone numbers and invited the ladies to stop by any time. We shopped throughout the house, sampled gourmet soups and fine chocolates, and enjoyed a glass of wine while visiting in front of the fireplace. We had all traveled through our lives to reach this moment of collectively sharing a good time as grown-up, sassy women.

I guided Maria through the shop, placing her hand on

items as I described them. She shopped for just the right gift for her daughter-in-law, who liked birds. I carefully placed a beautiful porcelain cup covered with painted birds into Maria's hands. She enthusiastically said it was just what she was looking for. At the check stand, she examined the rim of the cup. "Do you have another?" she asked the proprietor. "This one is flawed." It was indeed, but I hadn't seen it. Maria's hands were trained to see what her eyes could not. The proprietor exchanged the cup for a perfect one.

A month later, Maria met with the Red Hat Tamales for lunch at a bed and breakfast. In keeping with Red Hatters doing whatever they wish, we decided to eat dessert first, a rich chocolate cake. Later, while we enjoyed the chicken salad, Maria offered to hostess the next event, an Italian lunch at her apartment.

At our next meeting in her tidy apartment, I noticed that it was filled with photos. Maria kept her loved ones nearby, even though she couldn't see them. From her kitchen, the aroma of Italian spices filled the air. The table was set. Wine was poured. Maria, in her apron, stirred the steaming pot of marinara while she visited with her new friends. She knew her kitchen well, reaching here and there to just the right spots for whatever she needed to prepare our feast. Baked ziti, homemade meatballs and Italian sausages were delivered to the table, taking their places alongside a crisp salad of bright reds and greens and warm garlic bread. A homemade cheesecake swirled with chocolate sat off to one side, teasing us.

We women laughed, visited and ate too much! As we left, we patted our full stomachs and hugged Maria in thanks. She looked at us with eyes that had been blind since she was nine years old.

"It was my pleasure having you beautiful ladies as my guests," she said. "Now I'll just have to get a red hat before we meet again. I look really good in red."

Tawdry Behavior

by
Laura Farkas

For the first time in the two-and-a-half years of his existence, Mama's precious little man was spending the night away
from home; my eldest daughter had invited both of her little
brothers to spend the night at her apartment. With my other
daughter at a friend's, I was to be totally and completely alone
for several hours before the Hubs got home from work. I'd
been a bit under the weather lately, so I opted to stay in.

Given the rarity of the occasion, one might speculate that
I would be at a loss for ways to entertain myself during this
down time. *Au, contraire!* No picky palettes to consider meant
I could eat anything my little heart desired for dinner. I decided against steak (translation: I was too lazy to go to the store),
but homemade butternut squash soup hit the spot.

Delightfully satisfied, I nestled under my favorite Green Bay
Packers blanket, ready to enjoy the *NCIS* marathon completely

undisturbed. Perfectly content with just a few only slightly less than innocent fantasies about my favorite special agent, I stared at the screen with my good-girl status unmarred. Then I heard it calling to me from the kitchen. Like a ship following the siren song toward the rocks, I felt my body moving even as my mind struggled to fight the urge.

"No, I don't dare."

Yes, you do.

"I really shouldn't. What if somebody comes home?"

If not now, when?

I knew I was beaten. I gave in to my passion without so much as an ounce of shame. My eyes rolled to the back of my head in sheer ecstasy. Yes, I admit it. I've been involved in a torrid love affair with Ghirardelli chocolate for several years now.

It started out innocently enough, caving in to the flirtations of the occasional square from the splurge counter in the checkout lane. Before I knew it, I was hiding entire bags of the delectable delights in my dresser drawer, sneaking away to have one every chance I got. Morning, afternoon, the middle of the night; it mattered not. I simply could not stay away from my silky smooth tempter.

Soon I was searching for socially acceptable ways of spending more time with my beloved. The brownie mix allowed me to indulge my yearning under the pretense of providing sweet treats for my family. In public I appeared to be the devoted mother baking for her children, but in private I was a shameless tart who couldn't get enough. The double-fudge brownies were fine for the family, but when we were alone, I was all about the caramel-walnut brownies. I've even been known to bake both at once, hiding my sweet secret right under their noses.

So, there we were, Ghirardelli effortlessly leaving me begging for more and nobody around to stop us. I knew the consequences of my actions, but that's why God made elastic waistbands and empire cut blouses, right? When our time together was over, I quickly removed all evidence of our tryst and innocently met my hubby at the door, as if nothing had ever happened.

I should be ashamed of myself. A grown woman—a wife and mother at that—carrying on like a teenager with hypermetabolism. But I can't help myself. Someday my girth will give me away, but I'll deal with that burst seam when I come to it.

It All Depends

by
Nancy Withers

Menopause hit me fast! Everything I ate automatically went to my waist, my mood swings sadistically pushed me to see how high I could fly, and the night sweats began at dusk and ended the next day at 5:59 A.M. Other symptoms came on with the same vengeance, like my memorable moment at the grocery store after a mega-emotional day at work.

As was my habit, upon entering the store, I obeyed the sign, "Start with a Cart." With shopping list in hand, items arranged in my usual path through the store, I dashed off, hopeful to complete my appointed course without having to wait too long at checkout.

Please, God! I thought to myself, *Let me grab and go without meeting anyone I know, or who knows me.* It had been a horribly hard day and my moodiness was elevated due to many frustrating menopausal moments.

My basket began to fill with toilet paper, Kleenex and paper towels. As I paused to check on the sale price of kitty litter and designed cat food, I got that all-too-familiar feeling. *OK, stand still. Hold on. Ignore that tabletop water feature at the end of the aisle.* As I lifted a 20-pound bag of kitty litter, the urge instantly became too strong. *I gotta go! I gotta go right now!*

Taking a deep breath to get my bearings, and to also avoid an accident, I did a U-turn to the back of the store. *Please, God, let there be an open stall*, I prayed. I parked my cart by the stand of old lady canes and waddled through the door to the women's restroom. God must have been listening, as the restroom was empty.

I took care of my business then returned to my waiting cart. *Now, where was I on my list? Pellegrino, ah, straight ahead on Aisle 4.* I picked up three bottles and added them to the cart. Pushing onward, I wasn't but halfway up Aisle 4 when that light bulb went off in my brain—AGAIN! I had this sinking feeling that bladder control was becoming both a menopausal and an aging issue, which was apropos considering I was surrounded by disposable diapers, feminine hygiene products, incontinence supplies and bottled water.

Feeling like my security depended upon my poise (sorry for the play on words), I knew it was time to check out the grandma diapers. I looked both ways first to confirm I was alone, and then pretended to look at the Pampers, which were next to the incontinence products. I became confused studying all the products and had a hard time deciding which one to try. *Which is better? Super absorbent, ultra long, light pads? Or adult pull-ups that fit and feel like underwear? Or adjustable ones with and without buttons? How about worry-free with odor control? And what about the all important disposable? Do I need super, long or special blue lining? What's with this product that can be used by both men and women?*

Thoroughly confused, there was no way I was going to ask grocery staff for help selecting the right diaper! I almost settled on getting the Poise pads, but they didn't have wings, which I preferred. Exasperated with not knowing what to purchase—but more so because I had to purchase these things in the first place—I decided to return later that night just before closing. *Good plan! I can get the 40 pounds of kitty litter, then bury the Poise pads beneath it!*

I exited Aisle 4 and headed for the deli. Too late to cook dinner, so I picked up a rotisserie chicken and some potato salad, and then headed for checkout. I did return later to finish all my shopping—and I mean *all* of it.

Each night, I prayed that my menopausal body and soul settled into a more serene routine, one without valleys, hills or even those constant waterfalls. Ten years later, it has, and I'm thankful. But we all know that when you're a woman, anything can happen when it comes to our bodies and the unexpected—it just all depends!

Will He
Notice Me Then?

by
Sandie Lee

You gotta love those magazines made for the twenty-something crowd. The articles in them are ludicrous and some should come with a brown paper cover.

If truth be told, I guess I'm sort of a prude. I wasn't brought up in a household where S-E-X was discussed openly and freely, unlike said magazines that show mother and daughter laughing gaily over a mocha latte while they trade the latest techniques for pleasing your man. Heck, even the television programs of my era didn't showcase the love scenes—all they showed was a man with that come-hither look in his eyes as the woman obediently follows him into the bedroom, the door closes . . . *fade to black*. They could have been playing Monopoly in there for all we knew, and according to my mother, that's exactly what they were doing.

So when I recently came across an article stating the eight things a man instantly notices about you, I just had to respond:

1. How thick is your hair?

Apparently, thick lustrous hair means you're healthy. What about pulled back tight, unwashed for a few days, with something sticky clinging to the greasy tresses? Will he notice me then? If not, I'm sure I'll make an impression when I take the ponytail holder out and several strands come with it.

2. Is your smile genuine?

'Cause men love those little crinkles your eyes get when you're grinning—it means you're relaxed and fun! No, honey . . . it means I'm old and tired—they're called "CROW'S FEET!" And the grin is probably more of a psychotic episode being brought on by raging hormones.

3. The size of your group.

Big groups scare men off. If there are just two of you, he figures you won't abandon your friend; three is perfect. Great. So when I'm out in the grocery store with my niece's two screaming kids, feel free to come on over!

4. The pitch of your voice.

A higher register signifies youth and your ability to reproduce. Perfect! I'm sure my voice was in a very high register when I was yelling at the kids to stop climbing up the shelves in the cereal aisle.

5. Your hip-to-waist ratio.

Meaning your hips should be bigger than your waist (hour glass) for reproductive purposes (of course). And here I was trying to get rid of that sexy spare tire. Goodbye, Spanx. Hello cookies!

6. Your glowiness.

A radiant complexion means you have good mental health. No, it means, *I'm having a hot flash and the mood swing is sure to follow. Approach me now and I'll probably bite your head off . . . or cry . . . or both.*

7. What's fake about you?

Are you using fake nails, eyelashes or hair extensions? Guys will notice and perceive you as high maintenance. I guess the tummy-tucking underwear that's cutting off my circulation—but promises me that hour-glass figure for fertility—is a no-no? Thank goodness, these Spanx are killing me! Hmm . . . I bet I could recycle them into a floatation device.

8. Your eyes.

Men focus in on your eyes more than anything. What if they're all blood shot from the mood-swinging-crying-jag I had in the cereal aisle, with mascara streaming down my face like little black rivers?

I guess the good thing is, ladies, according to this article, we could basically be bald, hanging out with or without a number of people, have the voice of an 80-year-old, be a life-time smoker, have the body shape of a pear, have noticeable flaky skin, and dispose of all those tummy-tucker garments, just as long as our eye makeup is dramatic. However, you'll still have to remind him your eyes are not located on your chest.

Sandie

CHAPTER SIX

Stand Up!

We woman are always right, remember?

Your Hard Drive's Corrupted

by
Sylvia Bright-Green

The only thing my husband, Gene, and I knew about love was that it was spelled S-E-X. And the only thing Gene knew about sex was what he learned from high school and other equally uninformed buddies. Therefore, whenever my husband wanted sex, he would mouth a naughty little jingle to the melody of, *I'm Looking Over a Four Leaf Clover*. His fractured words to that song were:

"I'm looking under the skirt of wonder,
where I have looked before.
First comes the ankles,
then comes the knees,
next comes the panties,
and ah what a breeze.

There's no need explaining
the one remaining,
as it's something that all men adore.
So I'm looking under the skirt of wonder
where I long to look evermore."

Gene's other favorite ditty was: "Oh, she jumped in bed and covered up her head and said I couldn't find her. But I knew damn well that she lied like hell, so I jumped right in beside her."

That was about as far as Gene's romantic side went. Whenever I wanted sex, he wasn't in the mood no matter what romantic lengths I went through to entice him. To give an example—just before he was to return home from work, I would bathe, powder, perfume and put on my heeled boudoir slippers, slip into a short sheer-laced apron and position myself on his office desk. When Gene came through the door and observed me, he said, "What the hell's the matter with you? Get off my desk and put some clothes on. You're corrupting my hard drive."

Another time when our sex life had skipped a few weeks, I again decided to try a dress-up tactic. This time I put on a black leather mask, stiletto heels, fishnet stockings and a very short strapless cocktail uniform with scanty panties. When he opened the door, I had one leg slung over the back of the lounge chair. Next, I seductively danced around the chair and jumped onto it, doing a bump and a grind. He clapped and shouted, "Give that atrocious chair hell, baby. Stomp it, rip it, break it, so that I'm no longer reminded of it being a gift from your mother."

After that I decided life without sex is no life. I was so upset with Gene that I wanted to punish him, so I decided that if my husband couldn't come to my Mohammed then I was going to go a-mounting. That's when I got the idea to post a sign in a tattoo shop near my home. The sign cleverly read: "MAN WANTED, for a woman having a body like Europe, well developed and open to trade; an intimate nature like Spain, very hot, and a desirable place to visit; a disposition like Africa, wild, half-undiscovered needing to be tamed; a gentle aging like Greece, but still warm and desirable; and a spirit like Tibet, attractive and adventurous with a mysterious past."

When Gene came home and read my ad that I *mistakenly* left sitting on his desk, he went ballistic. He yelled, "What the hell are you doing?! If I ever find out that you cheated on me, hell will be paying you a visit. You understand?"

I yelled back: "Family jewels aren't any good if you don't have a secure place to put them. And by the way, whoever gave men genitals must have forgotten about the King Midas Touch syndrome where everything Midas touched turned to gold. Can you imagine him thoughtlessly grabbing his package to pee and how pissed off he must have been?"

Gene stomped from the room, which was his normal routine. That's why his threats didn't scare me, because if he was ever going to hurt me, he would have done it at some point during our 35 years of marriage. But he loved me, and I loved him. Furthermore, I never would have posted that sign in a tattoo shop. I only wrote it because I was angry and it was my way of getting back at him. Yet after his threat, I thought perhaps I should let him think he frightened me into *believing* his threat. So to settle the score with him, I decided to write a Living Will and also leave it in a readable place:

"I, Sylvia Bright-Green, being of sound mind and in a body of no sex, do not want to be kept alive by any 'artificial' means. And, under no circumstances, should my fate be put in the hands of politicians who only work for themselves, the judicial system where only the wealthy can get away with anything, the doctors who are getting a cut for every drug they push, or the lawyers who are interested in simply running up the bill.

"If a reasonable amount of time passes and I fail to ask for at least one of the following: my *toy* or a *Playgirl* magazine, and I have not been duly noted flirting with a sexy-looking intern, it should be assumed that I won't ever get better or that I'm already dead.

"When such a determination is genuinely reached, I hereby instruct my adult children and attending physicians to pull the plug, reel in the tubes and call it a day. At that point, I would then like my four children to call a New Orleans Jazz Funeral Band to come and do their theatrical thing at my funeral before I am cremated. Prior to the cremation, though, I would like my friends and loved ones to raise their glasses of Bailey's Irish Cream to toast the good times we have had discussing spirituality, food, men and sex.

"HOWEVER, if I should by any chance live, but need special care, I heard that in Ireland they have a nursing home with young, sexy, gorgeous-looking male attendants. These woman patients, I was informed, are happier, have regained their zest for life and made a rapid recovery. Therefore, my beloved family, if you really, truly love me, take me there IMMEDIATELY."

Signature: *Sylvia Bright-Green*
Date: December 19, 2011

After writing my will and Gene reading it, I got lucky. It turned him on. As a result, I am now writing Living Wills to support us, with Gene calibrating all the punctuation. And wow—can he punctuate!

Three and I'm Out

by
Kathleene Baker

"Darn, Robert Redford isn't quite as cute as he used to be! I just hate that." And I was adamant. It had been years since I'd seen Mr. Redford and didn't expect such a drastic change in his appearance.

My husband, Jerry, and I were watching him being interviewed on television. A true sense of melancholy came over me when I realized he was no longer a young and handsome hunk. I much preferred to remember Redford's striking face in movies such as *The Way We Were* and *The Sundance Kid.*

The interview continued, but I only heard a few words here and there. My thoughts had turned to aging. If age could take a toll on the likes of Robert Redford, none of us were immune. Just how many people—men or women—are blessed with such terrific looks to begin with? If it could happen to him, we were all doomed—should we live long enough.

When the program ended, Jerry spoke up. "Well, you

know, none of us are as cute as we once were." He was so nonchalant that I was caught completely off-guard. I sat on the foot of the bed in a daze and thought how much I despised those words.

Then it was time for my all-but-rehearsed and often-spouted spiel of how I didn't feel any older—it's all a state of mind. We bantered back and forth, all in good fun, for several minutes. Just as I began to stand up, dear hubby made a very disturbing announcement: "Kathy, do you realize this year you will be twice the age you were when we met?"

I felt like someone had hit me right over the head with a cast-iron frying pan! I fell backwards onto the bed, covered my face with my hands and recall uttering a few sounds of agony at Jerry's uncalled-for remark. There are some things that shouldn't be said to a woman and/or wife! What was he thinking anyway?

I began doing some quick math in my head. Not liking the first results, I ran through the numbers again—the results were the same and they sucked!

"Oh, darn—you're right, Jerry! However, that's the worst thing you've ever said to me in our entire married life," I shrieked, and I shrieked loudly! "I can't believe it. Don't you know when to keep your mouth shut? There are certain things best kept to yourself, and I suggest you remember that in the future! What is wrong with you, anyway?"

He didn't say a word, but looked at me strangely. Perhaps he thought I was losing my marbles? Or perhaps he was afraid to say one more word!

Still, I kept wondering; where did the years go so quickly?

It didn't seem possible! I went to bed that night still obsessing over our conversation and Jerry's dim-witted remark. I tossed and turned! I flipped and flopped! Secretly, I hoped all my writhing about was keeping dear hubby awake as well. It was hours before I drifted off to sleep. Being twice the age of anything is a horrid thought, unless you're lucky enough to still be under the age of, say, 15. What might be next? Would Jerry someday tell me I'm three times older than when we met? That could prove to be dangerous and I hoped he knew it.

I finally decided to look at the bright side of things before this revelation made me crazy. And after several days, it finally struck me! Indeed, a bright side did exist. According to statistics, Jerry will probably never be able to say such a thing. Since he's six years older than I am, he will more than likely already be six feet under! If, by chance he isn't, well, all I can say is he'd best never utter that dreaded *three* word. Should he do so, I'll be moving out.

Yes, it's as simple as that—*three* and I'm out! I'll pound on that call button as fast as my old, stiff fingers will allow. When the entire convalescent staff storms our room in panic, I'll demand they wheel me into the home's administration office. And then I'll demand a private room in a different wing—next door to Robert Redford.

For Your Convenience

by
Tina Traster

I'm scared about tomorrow. Waiting is the worst part. The closer it gets, the more unhinged I become. I try to stop picturing it. At least I've kept myself from Googling.

Since I scheduled the appointment two weeks ago, I've tried to press the thought into the farthest corner of my mind. There is nowhere in my mind for the thought to hide. Instead, I count down in my mind: *Twelve more days . . . 7 days . . . 36 hours . . . this time tomorrow . . .*

My gynecologist discovered it at my annual exam. "It's not a big deal," he said. "I see these every day."

My gynecologist could not pick me out of a lineup. He would not know my name if he didn't glance at my chart before an exam. I have seen him once a year for the past decade, but ours is a shallow relationship. *Routine exams.* He ticks off answers to my questions on a yellow pad. "No surgeries." "No medications." "No pain with intercourse." Sometimes he asks the same question twice. *Can't figure out if he's absentminded or trying to trick me.* He always asks, "How's your better half?" just as he cranks open my vagina to insert a long swab.

This was the first time a checkup veered from routine.

"There's nothing to worry about," he said, seeing me turn green as a kid stumbling off a carnival ride with undigested lunch in her belly. "Take your time," he continued. "Think about it. It's not urgent. I'm just suggesting you do this for your convenience."

Out of the room he sailed, leaving me and my gooey genitals in a paper robe with a swath of invisible fuzz wrapped around my head, trying to make sense of his words. "In 99 percent of the cases, it's benign . . . I'm not worried . . . it should stop the long stretch of mid-term bleeding."

And then his last words: "Just suggesting you do this—for your convenience."

"FOR YOUR CONVENIENCE." I fixated on those three words. *For your convenience!* I imagine a butler, tipping forward from the waist, saying as he hands me an umbrella, "Here you go, madam. Your bumbershoot—for your convenience."

Leaving the office, I called my husband. "I have a polyp on my cervix!" I shouted into my cell phone, yelling over the Fifth Avenue bus's squealing brakes. "The doctor says it's not serious, but he thinks I should have it removed. For my convenience."

"You're breaking up," he said. "I'll see you in a few minutes."

Crisp autumn leaves swirled on the ground. Tree limbs were thin with nakedness. I stood in the bus stop motionless, me and my polyp. I'd let two buses go before I placed that call to my husband on my cell phone. I didn't want to say aloud, *I have a polyp,* while riding on the city bus. Even though it is not a medical term, you still need to whisper.

My husband knew a gynecologist. "Can you please ask Michael to tell you all about this procedure," I requested that afternoon. He placed the call for me and learned that it was "like having a scab pulled off."

"Did you ask him if it was painful?"

"He said they numb you; it's like going to the dentist."

That was not the best image for me. When I was 17 years old and riding along with my mother on the Belt Parkway to a clinic in Manhattan, she said something I will never forget. While she was driving, she glanced over at me—sheet-white and quivering—and said, "Think of it as a dental extraction." My mother was not one to fabricate, but let me tell you there was nothing about climbing on a table and putting your legs in stirrups that is similar to the dentist. The searing pain from the injection that started in the vein of my hand traveled like a cigarette burning down to ash. I was too young to become a mother, but left with sadness nevertheless.

So I've been told that tomorrow's procedure is "no big deal" and really it's just "for my convenience." But still, I envision being cranked open like a soup can and ladled with clunky metal tools. It makes me think about the women in my family. My grandmother's mother who died in childbirth. My grandmother who lost a breast. My mother's carved-out uterus. My sister's tangled fallopian tubes. My womb.

The sun is going down. The sky is orange and red and purple.

It looks like a beautiful serape floating outside my window. Sometimes I think if the sun never set, I would never be afraid.

Twelve hours to go.

Give a Woman a Gun

by
Sallie Rodman

"Oh, damn!" I yelled, as the toilet in my bathroom wouldn't flush. I thought of that great line from the 1985 movie *Murphy's Romance* starring Sally Field and James Garner. Garner—playing Murphy Jones—says, "It's probably the ball cock. Most problems start there."

I knew it was going to be a struggle to get the toilet fixed. I'm not saying that my hubby isn't handy, but let's face it, Ed's no James Garner or Bob Vila. Oh sure, he has a garage full of needle-nose pliers, crescent wrenches and duckbill snips, not to mention a 44-piece screwdriver set complete with Robo Grip. How do I know? I've seen the charge bills. A card-carrying member of the Craftsman Club, Ed would rather nap on his day off than use an Allen wrench. He watches all the home improvement shows, nodding and saying, "I could do that." Yes, he could, but does he? Not really.

The toilet sat for four days, held together with a glob from my glue gun. Ed promised to take care of it on Saturday. I applied more glue and counted the days until the weekend.

The next day I had lunch with my friend Clare. I asked her, "How do you get John to fix things like plumbing problems in the bathroom?"

"Well, I lay out all the tools like we're doing surgery," she explained. "Then I put a nice piece of carpet or comfortable padding down so his back won't get kinked. He wants me to be there to keep him company, or for moral support, I'm not sure which. I grab a good book and read while I hand him pliers or a hammer. I occasionally nod and say things like 'that's great' or 'good job, sweets.'"

Wow, that sounded like a plan until she explained they hadn't had hot water in their downstairs bathroom for three years.

Just to be sure my hubby would get to work, I stopped at the plumbing store to buy the offending part. I checked to see that we had a soft carpet piece for Ed to kneel on, or for me to pray on, if needed. I made sure the pliers, a hammer and a saw were handy. Hey, what did I know? Tools are tools.

Saturday arrived and I awoke with hope in my heart. Around two o'clock, I made a stern announcement that the honey-do list was still lying untouched on the kitchen counter. Ed jumped into action and headed for the garage. He was back in the house in a flash.

"I can't find anything—those kids have been in my tools again!" he complained.

"Honey, the kids moved out a year ago," I replied.

With that, he went back to the garage, mumbling as he walked.

Several minutes later, Ed was back complaining he didn't

have the right size wrench. I told him to check his four tool chests again—there must be one in there somewhere. Finally, resigned to doing the dastardly deed, he miraculously found the proper size. I listened while he talked to himself as he strained to take apart the offending unit.

"Basketball game starts in 15 minutes. We could miss the tip-off," he said to no one in particular except our dog. I could have sworn I heard the dog let out a moan.

After about 10 minutes of grunting and groaning, Ed called me into the bathroom and explained the problem. It sounded like a foreign language, something about how the doober-dauber part was stuck in the thingamajig and he just didn't have the right tool to extract it.

"Won't a saw work?" I asked. He looked at me wide-eyed as if I had suggested he run naked through the neighborhood.

"You just don't understand."

"Oh, yes, I think I do," I said. "You want to buy that blow torch you saw in the Craftsman ad."

"Yeah." He smiled with a faraway look in his eye then promptly headed out the door for the store.

Well, do I have my toilet back? Of course. Did Ed fix it? Of course not. It seems Ed popped into the home improvements department on the way out of the tool department and now we're doing a complete bathroom remodel. As for the toilet, well, the glue glob is still holding.

Give a determined woman a gun—even a glue gun—and she can do anything.

The Price is Right

by
Ruth Littner

There was so much dust on my red carry-on bag that I was reminded of our family's financial crisis. I took the bag down from the closet shelf anyway and began to fill it with the clothes, make-up and medicine that I would need. I lied to my husband of 30 years about where I was going. I was running away.

Granted, it was just for the day and with my girlfriends, but in an odd way I felt as if I were cheating on him. I would be meeting up with women who would make me feel worthwhile and accomplished and funny and beautiful. My friends Chris and Bernadette are remarkable that way. I feel at ease when we're sipping wine, discussing great classics or talking about Bernadette's grandkids. I was leaving to take a breather from my daily concerns—for that day, I would not have to worry about the things I was leaving behind.

I told Jeff that I planned to go to a writers' think tank and that I was getting paid. He believed me, which made me feel guilty. Sort of. I told him this lie because he worried about money, and rightfully so. I was recently laid off and he has been in a precarious career situation, so we were watching our dollars very carefully. When I worked per diem, I imagined that he breathed easier than if I said, *Hey, I'm going to the beach . . . you work hard while I play.* But I felt OK about telling the lie because I needed to rest. While he sees the dark in everything, I am an optimist. Optimism may not get me anywhere, but I don't always have a dark gray Eeyore cloud hanging over me.

When I arrived at the Amtrak vestibule at 30th Street Station, I grabbed my ticket to Atlantic City and looked around the station, knowing I had a full 10 minutes. The interior of the immense structure was magnificent—gold leaf on the ceiling, 15-foot Art Deco light fixtures dangling like Damocles' swords, and carved alabaster railings leading down to the caverns where the mammoth trains waited for passengers in a never-ending circle of entry and egress through their portals.

Once on the train, I chose a window seat so there would be enough room for my red bag to sit next to me. As the train conductor broadcasted the few stops we would be making along the way, I got an electric feeling in my belly: I had control of my day and this excited me. The train lurched slightly as we began to move. The passengers were going to gamble and gambol, and I thought how lucky I was to be playing hooky. I proceeded with my usual solo routine—putting on make-up and munching on a packaged breakfast. The train gained speed and began a noisy but steady hum-hum-hum of rhythmic travel. With my iPod, cell phone and laptop, I felt wired and connected. I couldn't wait to write a story about lying to my husband and a trip to the shore, but I got distracted when I glanced out of the window.

The train chugged over the Schuylkill River and I saw a solitary rower in a one-man scull pulling hard at his oars. He was elegant and his stroke was smooth as he drew the oars in consistent tempo. The scull left a symmetrical V-shaped wake of foamy water as the boat glided. We were back on land before I could find out if the rower had reached his destination. And before I could return to my writing project, my eyes fixed on the busy roadways, revolting garbage dumps and imaginative, multi-colored graffiti painted on bridge stanchions and burnt-out buildings. I sensed a connection to the children waving to the passengers at the protected train track crossing, and I wondered where they were going and if they wondered where I was going. I saw rail workers on a nearby track, inspiring me to sing about working on the railroad—out loud. The gamblers on the train half turned their faces to me as if to say, *Quiet down, we have very important gossip to spread before we lose our money.*

I turned on my iPod and it played a Celtic jig, which put a huge idiot grin on my face. As I started my story, barely typing a line about my dusty red carry-on bag, the conductor bellowed the astounding news: "Next stop, Atlantic City!"

The temperature was ideal and the blue sky looked like a work of art when Chris and Bernadette picked me up. We went shopping for dresses in Stone Harbor and I tried on 20 garments. In each case, they told me how beautiful I looked. Chris bought a pocketbook and wallet and was happy; Bernadette bought a chamois duck for her granddaughter. We lunched in Cape May at the Lobster House so we could see the ocean from the deck where we ate. We chatted about our writing, and then we gabbed about everything and nothing, and they really listened to what I said.

We walked to the shore and played in the sand along with some gulls, and we admired Mother Nature's work. Just sat. Just listened. Just sat and listened to the pulse of the ocean, the waves gently coming in and teasing our toes. I cleared my mind, no easy task because my mind is usually racing. I forgot that I had a cell phone. I congratulated myself on reaching my goal.

They drove me back to the Amtrak station in Atlantic City and on the train I thought about my day and smiled broadly. Yes, Chris, Bernadette and I had had a marvelous day, clinking wine goblets, sharing torched *crème brûlée* on the boardwalk, sitting on the beach and silently reflecting. We did some writing and some shopping. I did not make the money I promised I would make at the think tank. I did pay for lunch and train fare. I spent the day with good friends. And I decompressed and regained my sense of value of myself, and *that* was priceless.

A self-portrait

The Force of Eds

by
Sallie Wagner Brown

In 1971, just as I began to see myself as the feminine version of the next A.J. Foyt, my husband's job took us from Seattle to Pocatello, Idaho, where my fledgling racing adventure careened out of control.

In Washington, I had trained for driving open-wheel race cars in an amateur league for both men and women. On the track at Kent Pacific Raceways, I sat low to the ground in my little Formula Vee, barely peeking over the hood. The engine screamed and the smell of exhaust and hot rubber assaulted me as I watched the open wheels hug the wonderfully complicated, nine-turn road course. Every muscle, every synapse had to engage every moment. What a rush!

Winning a race didn't matter to me as much as the thrill of speed, of barely keeping a powerful car under control. Downshifting at the exact right point going into a turn, hitting the accelerator just before straightening out again so the car pulls itself into the straightaway, was gloriously intoxicating.

The only racing available to me in dusty, flat, little Pocatello was stock car racing on an oval track. Despite the stark beauty and intense sky-wide sunsets of the high desert, it felt like oxygen deprivation just to be away from the trees and the endless waterways I loved in northwest Washington.

Then I found a little blue Volkswagen Bug outfitted for stock car racing. She wasn't the sleek, low-slung beauty I was used to, but she had real heart in her retro-fitted Porsche engine. Hope flared in me.

Other Bugs competed in the Foreign Stock Division, all of them driven by manly men who barely fit inside the cockpit. My first race, however, was a Powder Puff event, meant for wives and girlfriends of the "real" drivers, but I couldn't resist. Of course I won easily, having had more training—and being more foolhardy—than my competitors. I tried really hard to feel guilty until I climbed out of my car, removed my helmet, and a young, blond hunky guy presented me with a little pink-trimmed trophy, kiss included.

In the pits, a few other women sat on lawn chairs or car fenders in their cut-offs and halter tops, laughing and drinking wine coolers with the pit crews and drivers. But none were racing in the regular events. I sat alone in my clammy, fire-resistant, blue-and-yellow driver's jumpsuit on the hood of my car, leaning back onto the windshield and watching the really big Chevys and Fords vie for position on the track. The Foreign Stock Division raced last.

Finally, the call for the Foreign Stock Trophy Dash! I swung through the window of my car door just like the guys, mostly because the door was welded shut for safety, but also because it's a really cool way to get into a car. Ask Starsky and Hutch. They'll tell you.

A couple of guys from the pit crews smiled and gave me the thumbs-up as I bounced along the pot-holed entrance to the track. The women mostly gave me the hand-on-the-cocked-hip message, but one did blow a kiss.

Only four cars were in a Trophy Dash, so to survive the race intact, I simply had to use my Go-Fast-and-Stay-Away-From-Other-Cars Plan. No one was more surprised than I when I won.

Victoriously, I stood at the finish line by my burbling, hot little car, with gritty helmet in hand, waiting for my trophy and kiss. The same hunky guy who did the Powder Puff awarding must have bowed out because finally a rather portly, graying driver from the regular stock car division grabbed the trophy from a passel of arguing men and walked toward me. He handed me the foot-high, red-and-gold trophy, and then after aborted attempts at a friendly hug, we shook hands, and he said, "You go, girl!"

In less than a week, and all in one day, my hopes and my euphoria faded fast. A guy named Buck called to tell me that, and I quote, "Wimmin can't race on that track except fer in the Powder Puffs," and hung up. Before I could choose between laughing or crying, a woman journalist from the *Idaho State Journal* also called to ask for an interview about the ruckus over my racing in the real event. *I remembered a few cold shoulders, but no ruckus,* I thought. And Buck wasn't a ruckus.

"I know what it's like to try to break into a man's world,"

she announced. "I'd love to interview you, tell your story."

"I really don't want to make waves. I just want to race my car. I'm not an activist." I regretted sounding so whiney to such a strong-minded woman who wanted to help me.

"Listen, girl, we have to stand up for ourselves. I know. I tried to do sports reporting in Chicago but couldn't get past the roadblocks." Her voice got louder, more strident. "I couldn't get into the locker room where the instant, important interviews are done, so now . . . "

"Wait!" I interrupted. "I don't want to be a cause. I told you—I just want to race my car."

The line was silent for a moment. "OK. Call me if you change your mind." She didn't sound defeated. She had probably guessed what was coming next.

I still had hope that Buck and his friends could get over their angst, all because a woman had beaten the guys in Guy Territory. They weren't going to get over it if I stirred up trouble.

I traded my morning coffee for a glass of red wine, just in time for yet another phone call, this time from a representative from the Pocatello Stock Car Racing Association who never gave his name. He had found a long lost clause in their bylaws that said women could not be in the pits during races. Dripping with transparent, faux sympathy, the faceless, nameless voice on the phone said, "You're a good driver. We truly regret you cannot race because of a technicality." He paused. I said nothing, just sipped my emergency morning wine. "It's out of our hands. If you can't get into the pits with your car before the race, you simply cannot race." Another pause. What? He wants me to agree? Just say it's OK, no problem? I finished the wine but said nothing, so he continued. "No discrimination is involved. It's simply a matter of following long-established rules." I laughed. He hung up.

I poured another glass of wine and called the reporter. I still didn't want to be a pawn in her mission to free all women from the bonds of discrimination—I just wanted to race my car. I needed local people, people from the racing community, to step forward, to be on my side. I needed her help sending out the call. No more. No politics!

She wrote a column that simply told the story of my disagreement with the Racing Association's long lost rule about women in the pits. She added a picture of me leaning against my car with a smile, nothing haughty, nothing challenging, just a frustrated woman who wanted to race her car with the men.

Full of hope and armed with more gall than good sense, I got my husband to drive me and my little race car on its trailer to the pits the next Saturday night. A line of five burly men tried to stop us at the gate to the dusty flat pit area. Three of them had shucked the tops of their one-piece driving suits so that the tops hung down from their waists in the back. Two of them had cigarette packs rolled into the sleeves of their undershirts.

"Just drive on in, please!" I implored. My husband hesitated, and then without looking directly at the men, slowly pulled the car trailer until they stood aside and we parked in an open spot in the bumpy field. He had joined the association because I, a woman, could not, so we had access to the pits, but he knew I wanted to do this on my own. He left me there and made his way to the stands.

I jumped out quickly and started unhooking the tie-downs on

the car. I heard someone coming up behind me as my car gently rolled off its trailer. I turned around.

"I'm not looking for trouble," I began.

"You go, girl!" My old man trophy guy had his hands in his pockets and smiled as he repeated the encouragement he'd given after my last race. Three guys with him nodded and smiled as they stepped toward my car.

"Oh. I'm so glad to see a friendly face." I dropped the straps I'd just removed from my Bug and wanted to hug him, but remembered the awkward moment we'd had before and put out my hand instead.

"Ed," he said, as he took my hand in his right hand, and then patted it with his left. I felt like The Force somehow was with me.

The burly men from the gate arrived. They gave Ed and his friends sullen but determined and stern looks as they stood, legs apart, arms folded over their puffed out chests. In a voice I recognized from our phone conversation, Buck growled, "Ed, you know the rules don't allow wimmen in the pits." He hitched his sagging driving suit up a little closer to his beer belly so he wouldn't lose it entirely and wiped his nose with a hairy arm. His friends mumbled nonsense syllables and leaned toward Ed.

Ed smiled, lifted his right hand slightly and replied softly. "And you know women have been coming into the pits for years, Buck." Ed swept the row of burly men with his eyes, still smiling. They leaned back.

Before Buck could come up with anything but a grunt, Ed signaled me to my car. I climbed in and tried to start the engine. It faltered then kicked in with a lovely roar. Ed and his friends surrounded my car and casually walked with me as I drove toward the track for a few practice laps before the racing.

It was not as much fun to race—to drive fast—surrounded by the ill will of scared, unthinking people. But after my experience on the track that day, with those guys going head-to-head over something that should have been so simple, racing my car began to carry with it a deeper meaning. I began to understand the struggle the reporter had recognized way ahead of me. I didn't like it when she had added a bit about my battling with the Racing Association to her article, but finally I had to admit it was a battle, and I had been naive.

I didn't realize until years later that willingly or not, I was part of a wave, a movement. All I wanted was to race my car, just as others now want only to marry the ones they love, to make their own decisions about having children, to be considered fairly for job opportunities, to make the same wage as others doing the same job.

May the Force of the Eds of this world be with us.

Come Rain or Shine

by
Cathi LaMarche

A black cloud has followed me for so long that I've deemed it a friend and named it Betty. I'm hoping she'll become a fashion statement and people will stop me and say, "Nice Betty. Where'd you get her?" So far, nobody has shown so much as a twinge of jealousy. I can't even get one of my family members to take Betty for a weekend.

I've tried to dump her several times but, unfortunately, she knows where I live. Forced to strike up a little deal, I informed Betty that she could rain on me as long as she allows the sun to break through every once in a while. This agreement has worked for the past several years. After every downpour, the sun peeks out for a day or two, just enough to save me from drowning. After all, the girl knows my limitations.

When I speak of Betty, I'm not talking about a puffy blob of turbulence. I'm talking about a tumultuous, havoc-wreaking ball of fury that has accompanied me since birth. It started with my mother who ditched the family when I was 14. Not that a teenage girl needs a mother's advice. Talking to my father about feminine products and dating wasn't that bad. Although later on he admitted the childbirth and breast-feeding questions knocked him off his game.

In hindsight, the whole motherless thing affected my judgment when it came to relationships. I failed to recognize the signs of a marriage that was over before it began. An astute mother would've warned, "Haven't you noticed that . . . well . . . he doesn't really like you all that much? He's just old and desperate." Betty could've leaned in close and whispered something similar, but she kept silent right through the divorce hearing.

A few years later came a tonsillectomy. Knowing that children tolerate this procedure with a Popsicle as a parting gift, I failed to view it as a big deal. What are the odds that my surgeon thought that slicing the facial artery was part of the procedure? Thinking I looked a bit too young for my age, Betty stayed on the medical disaster kick: heart surgery at 39 and four additional surgeries during my early 40s transformed me into a 47-year-old trapped in an 80-year-old body. But hey, I'm still alive.

And so is Betty.

Next, she delivered five teenage stepdaughters whose loyalty to their mother rivaled the Red Queen's army in Wonderland. Really, Betty, was that the best you could do?

A few years ago, I decided to counter Betty's dishing of misfortune by purchasing a good luck charm. A trendy boutique in

Cincinnati deemed the Woo dolls to be the antithesis of the voodoo doll. The salesclerk said, "Oh, this doll will change your life. Our customers swear by them." She instructed me to display the doll in my home to ward off bad luck with its positive, uplifting words stenciled on its whimsical body, lulling me into the hope of a fanciful life. Hung by the door, the doll would bless me with good fortune whenever I stepped into and out of the house.

The first month of sharing space with the Woo brought a car accident, followed swiftly by unemployment. I banished the Woo to the garage for a slight attitude adjustment. Shortly thereafter, I ended up at the neurosurgeon's office for a suspected brain tumor. Needless to say, little Miss Woo is still clawing her way up from the bottom of a landfill. Lord help me if she ever makes it out. In hindsight, I know how the doll got her name. I heard the distinctive "Woo! Woo!" before the freight train hit me. So much for trying to conspire against Betty. Luckily, that whole brain tumor scare was just her way of proving she wasn't so bad after all.

I've noticed that my best friends carry around their own versions of Betty. A club for the less fortunate, we gravitated toward one another like lightning bolts to water. Oddly, we've all accepted bad luck as a way of life. We don't envy the fortunate, but look upon the Bettyless as shallow people who cannot cope with the slightest inconveniences thrown their way. We have a special name for these happy-go-lucky people: whiners. Nothing's more annoying to those who face tragedy more days than not than someone whining over triviality.

"Oh, my God, my cocktail dress is missing a few sequins."

"Can you believe the bakery was all out of baguettes this afternoon?"

"My hairstylist went on vacation. Just what am I going to do?"

For some reason, while my hair thins from a drug that I take for interstitial cystitis, I lack empathy for the woman in the grocery line complaining about her bad hair day.

As I get older, I believe there are some benefits to being tailed by Betty. Let's face it, we're most intrigued by people who spend periods of their lives under dark clouds. Celebrities who pop in and out of rehab, authors whose memoirs tell of years of misery and musicians whose lyrics resemble suicide notes haven't done so poorly. Come to think of it, perhaps I need a bigger and badder Betty since I've yet to be recognized by the masses for my literary prowess.

To be honest, I don't know what I'd do without the old gal. I've gotten so used to Betty that, if she ever left, I'd probably call the police to report her missing. Fortunately, I've gained a few useful skills while residing beneath her, like self-reliance, courage, resilience and moxie. Not to mention, a highly-developed sense of humor.

While life can be harsh living beneath a black cloud, I remain optimistic for the second half of my life. Come rain or shine, I plan to face head-on whatever Betty doles out. I'll just pop open my umbrella and wait for the typhoon to pass.

Wait a minute. Is that thunder off in the distance?

Spam-in-a-Can

by
Sandie Lee

It's no big secret that men and women are two totally different creatures. Women think differently, feel differently and act
differently—and for the most part, as Martha says—it's a good
thing. However, there comes a time in every woman's relationship
that she wishes her man was a little less . . . *man-ish*.

As a woman, I can tell you from experience that Mother
Nature is not a female. There's no way a woman would put another woman through premenstrual syndrome, menstruation
or even menopause, for that matter. Of course, the hormone
changes to a man are unbelievable—if you can't walk it off or
rub some dirt in it, it must not exist. So when my hormones
start raging, tears are flowing and even the cat is hiding, Hubby still doesn't get a clue.

I was having one of those particularly bad mornings, having
been up most of the night with sweating, nausea and dizziness.

Needless to say, I was extremely tired and irritable. Hubby took one look at me and said, "You look like crap."

"Thank you." *Bite me*, I fumed to myself.

"You're white as a ghost, your hair's all flat . . . is it greasy? And your face is REALLY wrinkly. Are those crow's feet starting?"

"Uh huh." *Who asked you?*

"Maybe you should . . . "

"Maybe you should shut up before this crow takes her foot and kicks you in your bird's nest!" I snapped at him. I then grabbed my favorite blanket and curled up on the sofa to pout. Hubby tip-toed past me and fled to the shower to get ready for work.

It wasn't too long after that I heard a knock at the door.

Who could that be? I peeked out the window. CRAP! There in my driveway sat a delivery truck, idling. *It figures that package would come NOW!*

I quickly went through my options:

A) Pretend I'm not home,

B) Get Hubby out of the shower to answer the door, or

C) Suck it up. *How bad can I look?*

Not wanting to make a trip to the post office to pick up the package, and my earlier threat to Hubby's . . . err . . . nether-regions would not bring him eagerly to my rescue, I quickly tried to fluff my hair and straighten out my old, ripped sweat shirt by tugging it over my old, stained, pajama bottoms. *Please let it be the old fat guy . . . please . . . please . . .*

I looked through the peep-hole. CRAAAAP!

It was the young spiffy driver with the cool shades.

After a quick mental pep talk—*OK, I can do this. Really.*

Hubby exaggerates. I look fine—I opened the door. The driver was gazing at his sheet and said, "Delivery for Sandie." He then looked up and . . .

. . . FLINCHED!

He immediately composed himself and shot me one of his killer smiles. I grabbed the package, scribbled something close to a signature and slammed the door.

"Who was that?" Hubby asked.

Sure! Now you're here! "It was a delivery."

Hubby put his head down, sniggered and asked, "And you let him see you looking like THAT?"

I shot what I hoped was the killer of all stink-eyes to Hubby, tossed the package on the table and proceeded back to my safe-sofa haven. I could hear my life-mate still giggling and tried my best to ignore him. Of course, he couldn't let it go.

"You know what he's probably doing right now?"

"Who?"

"The delivery guy."

"Ah . . . making deliveries?"

"No. He's on the radio to the other drivers."

"And?"

Hubby gave me a sly look and said in his best over-the-radio voice, "We have a Spam-in-a-Can on Queen Street. I repeat: Spam-in-a-Can." He giggled at his own wittiness and left for work.

However, there is one distinct difference between men and women—we get even. So with a sly grin of my own, I rummaged through my kitchen pantry until I located my revenge. I then placed my find on a plate, added a spring of parsley and scrawled a note for him to find when he got home from work:

"I've gone out for dinner. Enjoy your Spam-in-a-Can."

Sandie and her present

CHAPTER
SEVEN

Never Again!

Once is enough . . .

It's a Wrap

by
Cappy Hall Rearick

I have spent the last hour being measured and weighed. Presently, my body is wrapped in wet Ace bandages from the top of my head down to my toenails. A big-haired woman is squirting foul-smelling liquid all over me and she looks as though she is on a mission from God.

According to Mary Grace, this is going to make me skinny, and fast. "It's minerals, hon. They penetrate the gauze, seep into your pores and release every one a them bad ol' impurities." *I'd just as soon let the bad ol' martini impurities stay right where they are,* I thought to myself, but my face is wrapped so tight that the Jaws of Life couldn't get my mouth open to tell her.

I roll my eyes far to the right and direct a killer laser look at Mary Grace, the Doodah Sister responsible for this afternoon of body torture. Actual tears are pouring down her face, which is the only part of her not sealed tighter than a bag of Fritos because she didn't want to mess up her makeup. She is moaning horribly loud. "Uuuuhhhh! I can see the Grim Reaper. He's standing right in front of me and the S.O.B. is grinning."

"Nuuuhh uuuhh," I croak. "Iiiissss ooooeee mmeeee."

Mary Grace quits sobbing and looks hard at what used to be me. "What did you say?"

Ms. Big Hair, looking bored, sighs loud enough to be heard in Alaska. I figure she's wishing it was five o'clock somewhere in the world. I know I am. "Your friend said, 'It's her, not the Grim Reaper.'" Then she grabs more wet fabric out of a tub and begins to slap it on my hips. *Underneath this embalming fluid-soaked gauze, I must be the color of a blueberry by now*, I thought to myself. I want so much to put my clothes back on and get the heck out of Dodge, but every time I try to talk, I sound like a stroke victim. *Why did I let Mary Grace talk me into this madness?*

"We'll lose weight and inches all in one afternoon!" she had promised before I agreed on going with her. "Georgette said she lost 14 inches her first time. She went from a size 18 to a size 6."

"Get out! What did she do, turn her body into jerky? And Mary Grace, who is this Georgette person you're raving about?"

"Oh, she's the owner of the salon and she's impressive."

"You've met her?"

Mary Grace squirmed. "Well, in a manner of speaking I did. We got acquainted over the phone." She eyed my look of astonishment and squirmed some more. "Well, she sounded nice."

As I think back about that conversation, Mary Grace's new best friend—aka Big Hair Georgette—hovers over my helpless body, and as much as I want to, it would do no good to scream. Her accomplice, the one with the biggest butt in South Georgia, stationed herself next to the only exit, obviously by design. If my mouth would only open, I'd offer cash money if they'd let us return to the real world while we're still alive.

Mary Grace groans again. It is a loud groan. I look at her out of the corner of my eye and see that she is way past ready to be humble.

"I'm begging you, Georgette," she whines. "Unwrap us and we'll leave quietly. Please, ma'am, don't hurt us anymore."

Ma'am? Did she just call Big Hair "ma'am?"

Georgette's jaw is clinched even tighter than mine when she yanks my arm and motions for me to follow her. I am way too terrified to resist.

"Stand up straight," she yells. "Straight, I said! You look like a pretzel!"

I am shrink-wrapped from one end to the other and she's telling me to stand up straight? I want to kill this woman.

"Now, go on over to that rowing machine," she orders.

Seriously? Seriously? I can't even blink my eyes!

Questionably, Size-Six Georgette grabs me by my other arm and drags my mummified body behind her. I have no choice but to follow. Neil Armstrong moved faster on the moon in slowmo.

My feet have been wrapped tight, and then covered in a baggie secured with a rubber band. My body impurities have collected inside the baggie and are squishing and sloshing with every step I take. *I'll never reach that freaking rowing machine.*

"Sit!" ordered Big Butt Broomehilde, who is now to the

right of me while Big Hair Georgette guards me on the left. *If I don't do what they say, I may never see my husband again.* Mary Grace lets out another window rattling groan; she's eyeballing the Grim Reaper again.

When I finally make it to the exercise machine, they order me to row in place for 30 minutes. My mind can acknowledge only two words: in place. If I were butt naked, I couldn't row for 10 minutes, yet those two terrorists expect me to do so while wrapped up like King Tut without his jewels. *Help me, Jesus.*

Suddenly, as if directed from above, nature provides an escape.

"Aaaa haaa oooo eeee," I croak.

"Why didn't you go before I wrapped you?"

I shake my eyes back and forth. They're my only moveable body parts.

"Well, you'll just have to hold it."

"Nuuh uuuuhhh. Gaatta goooo ooowwww."

Number One Dominatrix glares at me and I am not ashamed to admit that I fear for my life. "You unwrap her over there," she commands her sidekick, "and I'll have to undo this side, I reckon. Shee-it!"

Thank you, Jesus.

While the two of them are trying their best to snatch me baldheaded, Mary Grace stops moaning long enough to yell out, mind you, in perfect English since her face is the only thing free of gauze, "Me, too. I gotta go, too. I've got a small bladder."

It takes us 10 minutes to become completely unraveled

from the house of horrors, but less than a minute and a half to fly out of the door like our butts are on fire.

"Mary Grace," I yell through my clinched teeth. "I thought you said Georgette was a nice person! Would you care to define 'nice?'"

"I take it all back," she yells at me while frantically searching through her pocketbook for car keys. "Every last word. Delete! Delete! Delete!"

I can't accept that. "Those women in there are crazy, M.G. Certifiable. I've never been so scared in my life. They're probably members of a cult. I could slap you upside the head for getting us into this."

Mary Grace cuts her eyes at me and a scowl forms on her face. "You touch this body in any way, shape or form, and I swear on everything that's holy, you will draw back a nub. Now get in the car."

I know better than to argue when my nubs are threatened. We are both silent until we're out of sight of the torture chamber, and then Mary Grace looks over at me and starts to giggle. It's contagious. In minutes, we are both laughing hysterically as tears stream down our cheeks.

"I need a Kleenex," she says and pulls the car over to the side of the road so she can look in her pocketbook without killing us both.

"Ohhhh. What a day. Can you believe what we just put ourselves through?"

I shake my head. "No, I can't. And nobody else will either."

She immediately stops laughing and grabs my arm. "Don't even think about telling anybody about this, girlfriend. You hear me? One word and you're dead meat."

"OK, Mary Grace. I promise I won't say one word."

She's got nothing to worry about. Who ever heard of a one-word story?

Sitting Room Only

by

Janet Sheppard Kelleher

I could not, at any age, be content to take my place by the fireside and simply look on. Life was meant to be lived. Curiosity must be kept alive. One must never, for whatever reason, turn her back on life.

~~ Eleanor Roosevelt

Ahh, former First Lady, can you answer me this? What happens when a curious woman charters a fishing boat? I'll tell you what happens . . .

Being a landlubber, the first thing I did was phone the captain to ask if his boat had a poop deck. A female senior citizen with diminished bladder capacity thinks about things like this when embarking on an all-day fishing trip.

"Guess you think that's the bathroom!" he said. "Well, the poop deck ain't got nothing to do with the toilet, young lady!

It's called a head."

"Makes more sense to call it a 'butt' then, doesn't it?" I said. You can't let 'em get the best of you, even if it is a man's world.

Next morning, once on board and with the reassurance a head was available, I thought nothing of drinking a thermos of caffeine on our way to the fishing ground. While en route, I wondered to myself why they call it a fishing ground? *It isn't even on the ground.* Then I answered my own question—since fishing is traditionally a man's sport, there are naturally built-in oxymorons!

About an hour into the trip, the captain spied dolphins, sea gulls and pelicans. The spotting was a dead giveaway that baitfish were abundant. With that good news, the captain circled around a while to find the perfect spot to cast the menhaden net. Menhaden: stinky fish good for bait, oil or fertilizer. *Fertilizer. Bathroom. Bladder,* I mused. Then my old bladder, interrupting my rambling thoughts, yelled, *Too much coffee already!*

I crossed my legs till my eyes were bulging then made a mad dash—if you could call it a dash, it was more like an exclamation point—to the head. My mistake was not asking to see the toilet first.

Down into the belly of the boat lurked the misnomer, reeking of yesterday's seasick sailor. I realized then why it's called a head. It was just big enough to stand outside, bend at the waist and shove a head in to retch.

Picture this—there was a hatch pretending to be a door, whose threshold I had to step over then heave my body through. (Dare I say heave?) It was like forcing a Nerf football through the door of a dollhouse—I bulged out on both sides. After I squeezed past it and tried to stand, my 5-foot-3-inch frame banged into the ceiling. *Aaaarrrrggggghhhh!* I now understood why men simply deposited their pearls in the ocean. The world is their oyster anyway, right?

Once inside the head, I had about 4 feet of height, with only 12 inches—give or take an inch—directly in front of the potty. And the room was no more than 20 inches, from elbow to elbow, wide. *How dare that scallywag captain call this a bathroom!*

Not only was the bilge-sucking room smaller than my coffin will be, when I closed the door, it was suddenly as dark as the inside of my coffin will be. I could not see any light in there. Feeling like a mime, I palmed the walls in search of a light. I couldn't detect any source of light—no switch, no chain, nothing! I've heard it's better to light a candle than curse the darkness, but no candle and no light switch meant cursing was the only source of enlightenment I could manage.

Fumbling around in claustrophobia as dark as Davy Jones' Locker, I realized I probably had more freedom in the womb. I frantically reached for something to steady myself in order to peel down my fishing pants, which were way too snug and stubborn because of all the sweat and frustration, not to forget the tight quarters. But there was nothing to grab. So I faced the hatch with my ba-donk-a-donk in the sink and my head bowed as if in prayer and inched down my jeans.

I turned to straddle the potty without sitting on it—because I knew deep in my heart that a hundred gross men had been there before me, all with the aim of a drunken sailor—when the captain cut the engines. Then gigantic wakes started rocking the boat.

Desperate, I lifted the seat to provide a bigger target, and then braced myself steady by stabbing both elbows into the walls. That's when a huge wave hit, knocking my legs out from under me and thrusting my naked rear end right into the *unseated* toilet bowl!

Right there, with my tush in that bowl, I had an epiphany. I saw the light. I declared my belief in reincarnation and thought about changing my religion. *Next go-around, I'm going to be born with a pointer like a fisherMAN.*

Squirming out of the head and struggling to stand, I decided the drinks in the cooler would have to wait until the dock was in sight. For there stood a steady and pristine bathroom stall whose comparatively roomy size I shall never complain about again.

So, Mrs. Roosevelt, you say we must never turn our backs on life. You're right. And I'll add this: watch your back when it comes to a sea captain's advice, because fishermen are prone to exaggeration.

Only a Coincidence

by
Georgia A. Hubley

I must confess I was once a "re-gifter." It began 45 years ago, long before "re-gift" became a popular word in our vocabulary, after being used on an episode of *Seinfeld*.

In late October 1963 I received a beautiful floral silk scarf for my birthday from my Aunt Zoe who lived in Florida. Even though the scarf was lovely, it really wasn't me—I couldn't coordinate it with anything in my closet. However, a tinge of guilt rushed through me when I considered donating the scarf to a charitable organization.

Then several ideas came to mind. *Surely, someone else might enjoy the scarf, and since I live in the West, who'd be the wiser?* I reasoned to myself. Immediately, I set-up up a re-gift drawer in my bedroom dresser and tucked the scarf away.

Several weeks later, I wrapped the scarf elegantly and gave it to my boss at a birthday luncheon. After cake was served,

I watched her open the silver gift box, slowly fold back the matching tissue and carefully lift the scarf to admire it. She smiled, raised the scarf to her chin, brushed her cheek with the silk fabric, and said, "It's so soft, I adore the lovely blue and green hues. It goes so well with my navy blue suit. Thank you so much."

"I'm glad you like it," I replied, beaming, feeling smug and secretly priding myself in mastering the art of re-gifting.

Thanksgiving was only days away, and I was invited to join my husband and staff for their annual Thanksgiving potluck. I volunteered to make a pumpkin cheesecake for the occasion.

At noon, I arrived with cheesecake in hand. As I stood at the front desk in the lobby waiting for the receptionist to announce my arrival, a deliveryman handed her a birthday bouquet. "Thanks!" she squealed. "Oh, I love giant yellow mums."

After retrieving the card clipped to the arrangement, she shared the message with me—the flowers were from the office staff.

As I offered birthday wishes, she interrupted me, "They are so nice to me here," she said. "I also received a box of candy and a gorgeous silk scarf." Suddenly, she pulled the scarf from a silver box buried beneath other gift boxes stacked on the desk and draped the delicate silk fabric around her neck.

I managed to finally utter a feeble birthday greeting, but I was stunned. *Is that the same silver box, tissue paper and floral silk scarf I re-gifted? Of course not,* I thought, *it's only a coincidence.* I was grateful when my husband appeared a few seconds later and whisked me off to the potluck.

As Christmas neared, I took inventory of my re-gift drawer. I was amazed at the nice things I'd accumulated. There were two bottles of Tigress Cologne by Faberge that was all the rage, an assortment of trendy gold and silver chunky bracelets, and two simulated pearl necklaces with matching pearl-drop earrings. I wrapped and adorned each re-gift with ribbons and bows and crossed six people off my Christmas list.

Two weeks before Christmas, I attended my employer's holiday party. Since it was a small financial institution, the party was an intimate and fun-filled celebration. The highlight of the party was a white elephant gift exchange. My gift for the exchange was a fondue pot with matching tray and forks. The gifts ranged from exquisite to outlandish. And the great thing about this type of gift exchange was the stealing and the trading.

After dinner, we all pulled a number from a festive green basket. "Let the game begin!" my boss shouted. Since I drew number one, I was the first to choose a gift. Eyeing a box adorned with shiny foil holly wrapping paper, I untied the red ribbons and ripped open the package. I was dumbstruck, instantly; I recognized the silver gift box. For a moment, I was engulfed with a glimmer of hope. *Surely, it's only a coincidence.* But as I unfolded the tissue paper, there was no mistaking the blue-and-green floral silk scarf tucked inside. It was my re-gifted scarf!

The fondue set I'd brought was the most popular item stolen and traded that evening. But, to my dismay, no one wanted to trade or steal the scarf. At the end of the evening, I smiled, wrapped the exquisite scarf around my neck and vowed to never re-gift again.

I was certainly looking forward to my upcoming vacation during the week between the Christmas holiday and New

Year's Day. I enjoyed the time off, the hustle and bustle of the holidays and spending time with family and friends, but relished returning to my office in the village.

On the first day back from vacation, I arrived earlier than usual so I could read the correspondence and loan files that needed my immediate attention. When I entered the break room, I was surprised to find my assistant brewing a pot of coffee. "Why are you here so early?" I asked.

"I was hoping you'd be in early. I have no one else to talk to," she said

"Sit. I'll pour the coffee. What can I do to help?" I asked.

"Just listen," she said. "Maybe I'm being overly sensitive, but I need to vent."

Tears trickled down her cheeks as she shared her dilemma with me. On Christmas Eve, she received a re-gift from her mother-in-law. The re-gift was a pair of pillow cases that she'd hand-embroidered last spring for her mother-in-law's birthday. Then after the Christmas re-gift was opened, her mother-in-law had the audacity to exclaim, "I knew you'd love them, because you're so fond of handcrafted items!"

Waves of compassion and anguish for her situation washed over me. I wondered why the mother-in-law didn't appreciate her daughter-in-law's beautiful sewing, embroidery, knitting and crocheting skills she'd been taught by her grandmother. My thoughts reeled as I searched for words of comfort and wisdom, but none came to mind to console her. I choked back the tears and swallowed hard. "I am so sorry," I stammered.

"Thank you," she said and gave me a hug. "I just needed a friendly ear to listen to my tale of woe. My husband doesn't believe they're the same pillow cases that I made for his mother. He doesn't understand why I am so upset, because he thinks it's only a coincidence."

Without any deliberation, the very next day I donated the contents of my entire re-gift drawer to charity!

To the Brink and Back

by
Sioux Roslawski

This is a horrifying tale. For the weak of heart, skip to the next story. However, if you are brave enough to consider buying Pajama Jeans or a Snuggie, or if you're even contemplating purchasing a Gut-Butt Dickey, perhaps you will not be permanently scarred after reading about my *hair-owing* experience.

It all began because of my Russian-born hairstylist's slick tactical skills when it comes to money. She is determined—during each of my appointments—to jack up my bill. For example, in addition to the $20 cost of a standard haircut, a shampoo is an additional $5 and a blow dry, yet another $5. The cost of a professional dye job, you ask? I'm not sure, but I shudder to think how much that would add to my tab.

As an elementary school teacher, stretching my paycheck is essential—an extra $5 spent here and there has an impact on my monthly finances. But Natasha has always bullied me to get my hair washed, to the point of luring me to the vicinity of the salon's sink, with a bubbling pot of borscht nearby and a television set playing *Dr. Zhivago* on a non-stop loop. I stood my ground—most of the time. Then I had an idea—my wily and cheap self will wash her hair *before* going to the salon!

Just yesterday, I made yet another haircut appointment for 5:30—after work. But the logistics didn't cooperate: a lot of gas would be wasted driving home, in the wrong direction, to shampoo my hair. And then I would have to double back to the salon. So that morning, before heading to work, I grabbed my shampoo and a towel to wash my hair at the school before going to see Natasha.

At 4:01, our school becomes a ghost town. At least on most days. Figuring I could quickly shampoo and slip out without anyone seeing me, I headed down the hall to the staff bathroom. Locking the door (it's a one-stall affair), I turned on the faucet and bent over the sink. I knew it would not be an easy task, since the sink was very, very tiny. Matter of fact, not only was the sink small, but the faucet jutted out quite far, taking more than its fair share of the sink space.

Prepared to possibly get into some interesting yoga poses, I began to get my hair wet. But to do so, I had to angle my head underneath the faucet, get one side wet, stand on my tiptoes and splash water on the very back of my hairline, and then pull my head out and repeat the moves on the other side.

Then something catastrophic happened. My head got stuck, wedged under the faucet, with no room to pull out and disengage. I was trapped. I turned my head to the left and tried to get it unstuck—no luck. I tried from the right side, but that had no effect either. While all this was going on, the metal of the faucet kept digging into and scraping my scalp.

Now picture this—three and a half hours later, the bathroom doorknob had been removed, the floor and part of the hallway flooded, a fire engine called, six firemen laughed their rubber boots off at the sight of me, and my principal was called back to work. But finally I was free. OK, in reality, all I ended up with was a scraped scalp when I finally yanked my head out on my own. But the idea of a bunch of hunky firemen coming to my rescue makes my fantasy version of this memory much more enticing.

From now on, I'll pay the $5 for that shampoo. Retaining my skin cells is worth it.

And Me
Without a Crotch

by
Rose Ella Putnam

My husband John, bless his soul, was a scavenger. Whenever he left our house with a load to take to the dump, I never knew what he'd come home with.

On one trip to the dump back in the 1940s, he came home with a treadle sewing machine for me. I took one look at it and groaned, but I couldn't say too much because my husband was so thoughtful, even fixing the belt so it would work.

The sewing machine wasn't its original brown color—it had been painted a brilliant blue. Part of the wooden flap that let the head down into the cabinet was missing, so it could not be let down. Even though the machine was such a color disaster, it actually worked!

When our first-born son Richard was old enough to start school, I made many of his school shirts with the sewing machine. And when our baby daughter Lexie grew out of her baby dresses, I whipped up some little girl clothes. But Lexie was so small that the patterns for 3-year-olds were much too big for her, so I'd sit her up on the table, pin a newspaper to her, and cut my own patterns. This was quite a feat in itself because Lexie was such a wiggle worm. I made many cute outfits, if I do say so myself.

To this day, Lexie still has a picture of herself wearing an outfit I made for her. When she was little, we took her to a photo studio and had a professional portrait taken of her wearing one special outfit. It was a white, pleated-skirt and brown-and-tan hound's-tooth-checked wool jacket and a beanie made of the two colors. Back then, material remnants to make such tiny clothes cost less than a dollar. "That was in the old days," my kids would always say.

I used this monstrosity of a blue sewing machine for years, until the day I decided to put a new crotch in my panty girdle, which we wore in those days. I cut the crotch out of a pair of pants made of rayon knit and attempted to sew it into the panty girdle. I happily sewed away, but when I picked up the girdle to admire my work, the crotch fell out. I was speechless! And crotchless! The feed-dog points on the machine that pull the material through were so sharp that they had just chewed up that rayon.

That did it! Right then and there, I went to town and into the Singer Sewing Company and came home with a new portable electric sewing machine. The machine was absolutely gorgeous, with the newest of this and that on it, and it was black! If I remember right, I paid $99 for it. Back then, that was a lot of money.

I was ready for my husband's judgment of my new unexpected purchase when he came home from his truck route. But when I held up my crotchless panty girdle and showed him the result of how frugal I had tried to be, he didn't dare say a word. I'm sure he was thinking plenty, though, as he hauled the good intention to the dump, never to be seen again.

No More Should

by
Lisa McManus Lange

I have deleted a word from my vocabulary. It was a word I used for too long, but with the help of a pair of running shoes, a giant waterslide and a milestone birthday, I have forever ceased to acknowledge its existence.

"Should." Small but powerful, this word ruled my life for many years.

Always hearing "You should do this" or "You should be like that" led to restrictive thoughts on my part, often preventing me from fully enjoying various life moments and opportunities. It was one thing to think that I should feed my children or I should wash the spaghetti slop from the cupboards, but it was another to always have that word hovering over me, always telling me to live my life how someone else saw fit.

Forced expectations and parameters set by generations before me about how a girl—and more so a woman—should carry themselves gave me a lot to live up to. Always hearing "you should" eventually led to consciously thinking and acting on the words without needing to hear them. "Should" had me doing what everyone expected me to be doing. As girlhood transitioned to adulthood, the word followed me, telling me how a woman, and then a mother, should be or should act.

Shortly after the birth of my second child, depression took over. Years of leading a life of "shoulds" and living up to others' expectations had taken its toll—I just couldn't keep up with the crap anymore. Sometimes I was able to free myself of that ominous word, but then guilt would creep back and squash that freedom like a bug. And with the depression I gained weight, and I didn't like myself very much. Others' reactions to me, especially of those who hadn't seen me for a while, were apparent. When someone called me "Fatty," a term I had never been called in all my previous 130-pound years, I realized it was damn time to do something!

During the early mornings, while everyone was still asleep, I power-walked. The walking turned to jogging, and by eating right, I began to lose weight. Over time, thoughts of "I *should* lose weight" changed to "I *want* to lose weight." I realized that my early morning exercise routine was exactly what I needed, and not just for my weight. The miles I clocked helped me figure out what I wanted to do with my life, not what I should be doing. With every step I pounded the snot out of that word— the same word that had dictated how I raised my family and how I raised ME. What had previously bound me and how I lived my life was slowly melting away with the pounds. Over time the depression lifted, and I continued to work to live my life without the word "should." That word wasn't going to control me anymore. But, as hard as I tried, it continued to creep back here and there.

Then one day I took my kids swimming and learned that my youngest son was finally tall enough to go down the massive waterslide without me. This came as a surprise to both of us, but one not realized until we climbed to the top of the slide together, like we had always done, and the attendant measured my son's height. Excited over his newfound freedom, my son went down the giant slide on his own. I turned to go back down the steps—since mothers *shouldn't* be riding down waterslides and *should* instead watch from the sidelines—when I suddenly thought, *Wait! I want to go down the slide!* And with that, I slid down after my son. When I got to the bottom, he was waiting for me, laughing and cheering me on! Even though I had been on the same slide dozens of times, always with a kid clasped firmly on my lap, this particular ride was the best I had ever had because "should" and "shouldn't" were left at the top. I instantly felt liberated from that stupid, dreaded word that had held me back for too long.

But the most poignant moment of that word releasing its hold on me was during my 40th birthday. Where others lived in fear of this number, I looked forward to it. With this milestone came a sense of freedom from anything "should." *To hell with the past, this is a new chapter—a new me!* I was getting too old to be bound and restricted like when I was younger. Time had revealed that I owned my life, and no one—no word—was going to tell me how to live it anymore. If I wanted to be fit, I exercised. If I wanted a clean house, I cleaned it. If I wanted a happy, independent life, I created one, for both myself and my family.

As soon as I let go of all those nasty "shoulds," I was free. My exercise routine, coupled with poignant moments like the waterslide and a milestone birthday, all had their place in finding my independence. When will you find yours?

The Windy Dress

by
Glady Martin

I once had this really pretty sundress I practically lived in each and every summer. It had all my favorite colors—water-colored flowers in pastel shades of green, blue and purple—and it complimented my complexion perfectly. Plus, it was very comfortable. Made with four meters—or more than 13 feet—of material, the dress was HUGE. Most women commented positively about it, but one woman called it "The Tent." But it was a very pretty tent!

While wearing this tent one day in my little Canadian town, I learned three very valuable lessons:

#1) Women should NOT go to the hairdresser

#2) Women should NOT wear big dresses

#3) The native meaning behind this sleepy little village's name of "place of many winds"

We'll start with Lesson #1: You know how we women get caught up in our daily lives of work, children, laundry, cooking and often charity work? Well, somewhere in the midst of all of these things, we sometimes forget to treat ourselves. I decided to do some charity work on myself, even though I had to pay for it. I was going to get my hair done.

I was looking forward to this special time, for me and me alone. Once at the beauty parlor, I lay in pure luxury as the hairdresser washed my hair, massaging my scalp into such a re-laxed state that I almost fell asleep. After a fancy trim and blow dry, the hairdresser began to work her magic with her tool of the trade—the curling iron! In all the years I have been using a curling iron, I could never get my curls the same as the ones she perfectly created and sculpted on my head.

Knowing I was in good hands, I closed my eyes and drifted off into a nice, dozy daydream of relaxation. When I opened my eyes, I was pleasantly pleased with the finished product. I paid in full and gave the young lady a nice tip.

Leaving the hairdresser with my new stylish and elegant coiffure-do, I felt like a million bucks. But before I reached my car, which was across the parking lot, my hair looked like I had been hit by a lightning bolt instead of sitting in a professional styling-salon chair! That darn wind had undone all my beauti-ful bouncy curls!

Lesson #2: When I finally made it to the car—with my hair now looking like a shaggy dog's head—I opened the driv-er's side door and reached in to retrieve some recycled shop-ping bags, as I had planned on going to the market which was in the same little mall. As I bent over, a lovely gust of the town's namesake scooped up all four meters of my dress and flipped it right over my head! Shocked, I bolted up straight and with flapping arms lost in all the material, I frantically tried to pull my dress back down and cover my butt up before anyone saw this horribly embarrassing moment. But, alas, I was too late! Because it was early afternoon, there were many people in the parking lot going about their business. It was impossible for any eye to miss this hilarious spectacle.

But then, I would have laughed, too. Picture a lady flailing wildly in an upside-down, multi-colored tent dress, with the only thing showing being her legs and the blue-flowered granny panties covering her big butt. Once she had her dress somewhat back into place, imagine the same lady with a bright red face and bizarre hairdo as she jumps into her car and drives off into the sunset, with no groceries.

And what did I learn for Lesson #3? It's hard to be a hottie in this little, beautiful, but windy place, especially for a lady wearing a tent for a dress. "Place of many winds" should be changed to "place of the laughing winds" because that's what Mother Nature did. And looking back, I can now laugh right along with those rascally winds. And, no, I have never worn that sundress in public again!

Glady

Hair Gone Wild

by
Stacey Gustafson

Everything I needed to know about hair I learned from watching *Charlie's Angels*. They say that your favorite hairstyle travels back to the time when you thought you looked your best. For me that was the 1970s, and my hairstyle of choice was called the "Farrah," after the late actress Farrah Fawcett.

The Farrah was a style I could figure out. Cool, feathered, moussed a mile high, curled up tight with an iron. I methodically worked on it each morning before high school, loading on gel, wax and mousse. I finalized the 'do with half a can of Aqua Net Hair Spray, thick and sticky. And I added a fake tan, orange streaks and all. *Voilá*, ready for school. The big hair look—no one could do it better than me.

But today—40 years later—my Farrah style was a bit more lax. But it is still there. As I was getting ready for date night with my husband, my daughter approached me in the bathroom.

"Mom, your hair looks so 1970s. Want some help?" she asked.

"I guess."

After having two children and lugging them around to 2,890 baseball games and more than 10,000 basketball practices for the last 17 years, I admit I've become a little lazy. I consider it fancy to put my hair in a ponytail and dab on lip gloss. And who had time for a blow-dryer?

My daughter combed, twisted, teased and sprayed my hair. After grooming me for 30 minutes, she turned me around to gaze at her creation. I was at a loss for words. Lady Gaga in her finest stared back at me, but without a long feather and a tiny black hat. Add a meat dress and I would be unforgettable.

"I think I can handle it from here. Thanks," I said, as she walked out of the room.

I needed to get current and break from my old ways. *I need age-appropriate hair,* I thought. With that, I scheduled an appointment to update my look.

"What can we do for you today?" the gal at the salon asked as she pulled back my hoodie and yanked out the elastic band on my ponytail.

"I need an update. Surprise me."

"But what do you usually do?" she asked as she massaged my head with aromatic oils.

Oh, we don't want to go there. I have been through more styles than Imelda Marcos has shoes. Remember the shag in the mid 1970s made famous by David Cassidy and Rod Stewart? Shorter at the top, downward layers in the front. Blow-dry upside down after loading on tons of styling gels, fluffy and full.

Or what about the perm? In the 1980s, I was treated to a home perm kit, courtesy of my best friends. Major frizz. Topped it off with an application of Sun In. Teased the bangs out, piled high with a scrunchie. I looked just like a poodle. Gob on gaudy jewelry to complete the ensemble. My friends and I looked identical.

Thankfully I never attempted the Dorothy Hamill or the female mullet.

My stylist tapped me on the shoulder to shake me out of my daze in order to witness her magic as she transformed my locks. For an hour, she snipped and trimmed, paying careful attention to my face, hair texture and life style. She did an awesome job fixing my hair, smooth side swept bangs and straight, glossy locks in the back. *A natural look*, I thought when I glanced at myself in the mirror. I liked what I saw.

"Thanks, I love it!" I said with a hug.

I purchased all the hair products she recommended. "I can do this," I said to myself. Once at home, I darted into the bathroom to check it out in my own mirror.

I admired the reflection staring back at me. But what if I just brushed a little here? Or curled a tiny bit there? Within

moments, my hair was fluffed, poofed and once again sprayed immobile. *Aw, much better.*

"Good morning, Charlie! I'm back. Miss me?"

(Top left) Karen Fick Moore
(Top right) Sharon Fick Wernig
(Seated) Stacey Gustafson

Sense and Sensibility

There's always a lesson to be learned . . .

Egged On

by
Terri Elders

"Tell me, too," I begged my sister. "Please!"

Patti, a year older and 3 inches taller, just smirked and shook her head. Earlier that morning Mama had dragged her into the bathroom, slamming the door in my pouting face. I had pressed my ear against the door, but could only hear Mama's hoarse whispers and Patti's muffled giggles. I felt so left out and bitter that I even turned down my baby brother's offer to go hunting for rotten eggs in the barn.

I tried again that night as we undressed for bed. "Nope, you're too little." Patti gave one of my pigtails a tug, tossed her curls back over her shoulder, and hopped into bed with a *Photoplay* movie magazine. I crawled into my own twin bed and picked up my book, *The Secret Garden*.

Everybody had their secrets, I concluded a little later, as I turned off the bedside lamp.

Two years later, my homeroom teacher announced a bit nervously that we would be having a special event that day. All seventh-grade girls were to go to the auditorium instead of to their regular fourth-period class. The seventh-grade boys were to gather in the gym. When we asked why, Miss Laird blushed and twisted a lock of her salt-and-peppered hair around a forefinger. "You'll find out when you get there," was all she said.

I glanced around the room and caught what looked like Patti-like smirks. Other girls avoided one another's eyes. It was early in the Nifty Fifties, and everybody seemed to be in on an awkward secret, except me. I had skipped third grade, so at 12 I was a year younger than others in my class. But I doubted that whatever it was they knew, and I didn't, had not been revealed back in third grade.

By lunchtime, I emerged from the auditorium, at long last in on the secret, too. What a surprise! I had learned I had tubes and eggs and would someday wear a white wedding dress. The animated film didn't quite relate how these were all linked together. And it didn't explain why Mama got mad when I asked her about the lyrics I heard to a song by the Dominoes called *Sixty-Minute Man*. But at least I had added a couple of new words to my burgeoning vocabulary: puberty and menarche.

God knows what the boys had learned in the gym that morning, but they shrugged their shoulders manfully inside their leather jackets and winked at each other over the franks and beans we were served in the cafeteria that long ago noon. From time to time one of the bolder boys would leer at us and call out, "Hey, are you a woman yet?" Then the rest would collapse in snorts and hoo-hahs and choke on their chocolate milk.

On Saturday morning I walked to the John Muir Branch Library, and while the two library clerks busied themselves at the card catalogue, I edged over to the adult 600 section, quickly pulled out a book on human sexuality and slipped into the tiny bathroom at the back of the stacks. I soon learned what the film and gym teachers had neglected to tell us . . . and why Mama got upset about that Dominoes' song. And I added a few more words to my rapidly expanding vocabulary list: intercourse, ejaculation, orgasm. I decided not to mention them to either Mama or Miss Laird. Of course I figured Patti had already learned these on her own and didn't need my help. If she hadn't, I wasn't inclined to share.

But two more years were to elapse before I had a special event of my own and found the tell-tale pink smudge on my panties that let me know I had started my period. When I went to ask Mama for a sanitary napkin and belt, she clapped her hands together, just as if I had told her I had won first prize in a Betty Crocker Bake-Off.

"We'll run down to the five and dime for that belt, but in the meantime, you can pin one of these pads directly to your panties." I heard pride in her voice, but wasn't certain why.

Patti cast me a condescending glance. "It's about time," she snickered. I seethed inwardly, once again one-upped. Patti had been getting visits from "Auntie Flo" for three years now. I had just finished ninth grade and would turn 14 the next week.

It struck me that maybe Mama and Patti didn't anticipate that I'd ever grow up, that maybe puberty was something not to be anticipated for girls who played kick-the-can with the neighborhood boys until dusk and served as referees for Girls

Athletic Club basketball tournaments.

As summer wore on, I worried about whether the thick pads would chafe me if I tried to play tennis when on my period. When I asked about the new tampons I had seen at the Owl Drug Store, Mama looked horrified. "Those are for married women, dear. Besides, you shouldn't be running around at all on those days."

That was also the summer I had my first boyfriend and learned that real kissing involved more than the quick pucker-to-pucker smack I'd previously had from the neighborhood boys when we played Spin the Bottle. So that's when my worries started.

I had read in that book I borrowed from the adult section that women had their periods at set intervals, just about 28 days apart, and that it somehow related to the cycle of the moon. So after the full moon when my second period did not arrive, I started to panic. I wondered if all that kissing with my boyfriend somehow had stopped my development. Or worse, had it made me pregnant? I remembered reading in that anatomy book that women ceased menstruation when pregnant.

Asking Mama was out of the question, and I certainly didn't want Patti to think I didn't know. So I had to sneak back to the adult stacks again. This time, though, my reference book was missing, and all I could find on the shelf was *Sexual Behavior in the Human Male* by Dr. Alfred Kinsey. I doubted it would contain anything useful on female menstrual cycles, but I smuggled it under my blouse anyway and headed for the restroom. Once again I expanded my vocabulary: cunnilingus, masturbation, sadomasochism.

Hmmm, I told myself, staring at the charts and graphs. *This growing up business is a lot more complicated than what I would have guessed.* I was relieved though when I could not find anything that said kissing was related to female fertility. But I worried that maybe Mama and Patti had been right, that some girls just never did really mature.

Fortunately, before I was forced to visit the stacks a third time, I finally had another period. This time when I saw the splotch, I breathed a sigh of immense relief. I had just about decided my eggs were as rotten as those my baby brother and I used to hunt for in the old barn.

In those misnamed Fabulous Fifties, the only rotten eggs turned out to be the teachers, parents and media censors who doled out only enough information to adolescent girls to confuse and frighten them. Those same rotten eggs perpetuated the myth that a female's menstrual cycle dictated who she was and what she could become.

Today I hear women lament the approach of menopause with the same anxiety that they experienced with the onset of puberty. "Fifty is the new 30," I read. Really? Do women still tie their value, their productivity and their femininity to their menstrual cycle? Are we still defined by our eggs? Over-the-hill flavorless stewing hens once our eggs shrivel?

Maybe we do not have to accept this myth. There is hope. I see the Baby Boomer actresses such as Glenn Close, Helen Mirren and Susan Sarandon—no spring chickens—continue to portray vibrant post-menopausal women in leading roles.

Moreover, the other night I watched a video with Meryl Streep tearing up the scenery as a flirtatious babe in one of the funniest hen parties ever staged—*Mamma Mia!*

Congratulations, Meryl. At 59, you're a woman! And at 75, free of fussing with tampons and calendar consultations, so am I—and still tender to the bone.

Die-Hard Eager Beaver

by
Mary A. Berger

Years ago, when the highlight of my day was vacuuming flower designs in the carpet, I knew it was time for a change. As a newly-retired woman, I thought there should be more to life.

"I've always wanted to make clay pots," I told a friend. "You know, carry on the work of the old masters."

"And play in the mud?" she teased.

"Yes, and I know the perfect place." Before my friend could say "mud pies," I was off to our local college where I signed up for a pottery class. Loaded with confidence, I felt certain that making pots on a potter's wheel would be a cinch.

On the first day, I was ready for the challenge. Dutifully, I listened as our instructor showed us how to knead our clay to prepare it for the potter's wheel. Meanwhile, the S.A.P.s (Smug Advanced Potters, I called them) looked on.

"Brute strength isn't necessary," our muddied-up leader

explained, demonstrating the kneading process. "Technique is the key."

It was time to get my hands dirty. I reached for a wad of clay and punched at it. Nothing happened. I gave it a hefty *kung-fu* whack to let it know who was boss. The clay seemed to stare back at me as if to say, "You've gotta be kidding."

But I persisted until at last the clay was ready to use. The instructor had us seated on benches facing our wheels. Then, with a flamboyant wave of his muddy hand, he ordered, "Throw the clay!"

I wound up, tossed the clay toward the wheel ... and missed. It went sailing into the lap of one of the S.A.P.s seated nearby.

"You're supposed to throw it *onto* the wheel," the young man rebuked.

So, my aim was off a little. After gingerly—and I do mean gingerly—helping to remove the clay from the young man's groin area, I started over.

A container of water sat alongside the wheel. We were to use it to help keep the clay moist. Reaching inside, I drew out a handful and dribbled it over the mound of clay. Then I set my wheel turning. To my surprise, the wheel got stuck on high speed and globs of mud flew out in every direction. Wouldn't you know it, at that moment the instructor came by, leaned over to give a few pointers, and got a face full of sopping, wet clay!

I cringed, while everyone within mud-slinging distance wiped themselves off. With clay still dripping from his face, the instructor headed the other way, shaking his head and toweling off his face.

Talk about embarrassing. Still, I was eager and determined.

My next glob of clay had a mind of its own. After veering sideways, it slid right off the wheel, landed on the floor with a plop, and stuck like a plunger. Blushing up to my eyeballs, I scraped it up with an old comb I found in my purse.

Things got worse.

We were shown how to center the clay and form it into a tall cone. My attempt looked, well, obscene, in a phallicky way, if there is such a word. So I sneaked over to the reject bin and tossed it in, hoping no one would notice.

"Not a keeper?" one of the S.A.P.s asked, strolling by.

"Uh, no, not a keeper," I said, throwing off the jargon with an air of confidence.

At last, in a surge of triumph, I slapped some new clay into shape like a pound of hamburger. What a thrill! I felt like Napoleon. But then I met my Waterloo.

A couple of S.A.P.s had wandered over to the reject bin. They were giggling and joking among themselves while holding up my discarded clay creation for the whole class to enjoy. Sagging, I wondered if I should've stayed home with my creative vacuuming.

But then, ever eager for a challenge, I perked up. Another class was forming across the hall: Glass-blowing!

Now that didn't sound too hard.

Single and Searching

by
Sara Foore

After a tumultuous relationship, I decided something needed to change. I was tired of the roller-coaster ride that always ended with me wanting to throw up. After giving myself time to get over the relationship, I decided I deserved to be happy.

I'm a fun-loving, thirty-something who had watched the majority of her single friends enter into the union of marriage. While I was successful and had accomplished a lot in my short time on Earth, I was ready to meet that special someone who would be my other half. The insanity that ensued would be the result of my decision to dip my toe into the world of online dating.

As a hard-working girl with an already busy social life, I thought, *Why not?* The thought of trying to find a mate via cyberspace was intriguing. What happened next was beyond my wildest dreams and became a source of entertainment. These chronicles are all true and nothing has been embellished. Why embellish when the real thing is so good?

Unless you've ever joined an online dating site, the idea of a profile is probably foreign to you. Please let me explain. Besides having to post the most flattering pictures of yourself while writing tag lines that say "Pick Me," you have to answer a lot of personal questions. In my case, I had to complete 300 questions, all in that quest to eventually match me with my cyber soul mate. I wondered, *Were they really going to be able to find me a soul mate based on how often I like to go out and what types of food I eat?* Silencing my cynical side, I decided to just go with it. What did I have to lose besides a silent rejection from someone I've never met?

It was only after I started receiving 10 emails a day, each promising that the match would prove even more exciting than the one before, that I started to question this whole idea. I have considered myself to be an accepting, kind person in the past, but this experience was bringing out my shallow side. *No wonder some of these people are single!*

With each email, I learned that certain things became definite deal breakers:

- Posts a picture of himself holding his cat = creepy
- Extreme close up where nose hair is visible
- Wearing a T-shirt that is way too tight, mid-fist pump
- Standing next to unidentified female who might be his ex
- Making an obscene gesture in the photo because, hey, who doesn't like that guy?

The person who said, "There is nothing to fear, but fear itself" clearly never had a blind date. There is a certain awkwardness that came over me each time I had to meet someone. I would get anxiety about having to find him inside of a bar or possibly approaching the wrong person. I found myself telling the guy what I would be wearing in order to avoid the look-away-and-look-back game, when trying to decide if you are the person they should meet.

My first date was a guy named Mike who, on paper, seemed my perfect mate. We met at a local watering hole and had a beer. When he asked if I'd like to have another drink, I thought, *This must be going well!* After the second drink, I told him I needed to get going and we left at the same time. He asked if I wanted to go to lunch later that week, and I agreed. I wasn't sure I felt chemistry, but I figured I would give it one more shot. When he didn't call or text the following night like he said he would, I assumed something was up. I then received an email from Mike stating he had had a really good time, but didn't think we were a good match. I sat there perplexed, half tempted to write back and tell him what a wimp he was for sending an email. As the minutes ticked on, my feelings about the situation changed. Although his method seemed weak, I had to give him credit for at least saying *something*! I've found over my dating career that many guys would rather just fall off the face of the earth instead of being upfront.

The next guy I went out with will be referred to as "C." I am leaving it as an initial because it is as mysterious as he was. C liked things on his terms and wasn't big on compromise. He wasn't a big fan of having a lady in charge. We didn't mesh well and it was a power struggle. C was a nice guy, but his life had more drama than all of my girlfriends, combined. The last straw was when my dog was really sick and C was upset that I couldn't go with him to get ice cream.

Mike and C weren't the only guys I dated from the site; there were many more over the span of several months. Online dating was a learning experience and it taught me a few things:

- I may be a control freak.
- I may not be ready to think of someone other than myself in a relationship.
- I may find something wrong with everyone.
- I am pretty fantastic and there are people who are interested in me.
- I need to start smiling more and acting approachable.
- I am not willing to settle because that's what society thinks I should do at my ripe age of 32.

So, if you're tall, have a sense of humor, aren't living on a friend's couch, have a stable job and don't cite your mom as your best friend—get in touch with me. And if you have a brother, cousin, friend or uncle who fits that profile, let me know—because I'm still single and still searching.

Dance Hall Girl

by
Ellen Denton

I've always considered the time-honored profession of the geisha as one of elegance, mystique and beauty. I'm also a curious person by nature, which is why, when I was in my 20s and job hunting, I became intrigued by an ad in the classifieds for a dance-hall girl. My wonder about such things overcame my better judgment, and a dance-hall girl I became—for three whole days.

A dance hall was where taxi-cab dancing was done. A man would select a girl and then punch a ticket at a subway-like turnstile as he brought her onto a dance floor. They would then dance, or instead, sit and talk while having drinks at the many tables placed around the dance floor's perimeter. The idea was for the girl to keep the man with her as long as possible, socially entertaining him with either dance or conversation. When he was done, he would punch the ticket at the turnstile on the way out and pay for the time spent. The girl received a percentage of that total.

I've always had a long-term fascination with Japanese geishas, the elite women who entertained men with dance, song, the playing of musical instruments and skilled conversation. The word "geisha" translates into "doer of art." So when I read the employment ad, I didn't visualize some dive with lonely, horny, weird guys punching a ticket to dance and talk to a pretty girl. Instead, I saw myself, with heart-stopping grace, pouring tea into tiny, porcelain tea cups. Truth be told, I had a fantasy I wanted to fulfill. And had I in fact been serving tea in tiny porcelain cups, had I showed up for work in a hand-embroidered, silk kimono, or had the dance hall been the Imperial court in Japan, it would have been just like that.

Fantasy aside, I arrived for the job interview dressed in simple white slacks and a white, sleeveless, high-necked shirt. The clothes were modest and understated, but fit closely enough to show off my body to advantage. The panties I wore had a large butterfly on the back, and since the white slacks were slightly sheer, the butterfly showed through faintly. I thought that was a nice aesthetic touch.

The interview involved little more than the owner of the establishment looking me up and down, asking me to turn around slowly in a circle, and when I came face front again, saying "You're hired." I'm sure that butterfly was the selling point.

He told me that I, along with other girls, would sit on a red couch that stretched almost the entire width of the room. Men would pay a cover fee to come in then stand a distance away behind a dividing bar, facing the girls, until they chose one to dance with. There was no sexual contact allowed and meeting the men outside of the dance hall was not permitted. If anyone did anything that the girl didn't like, she could signal the bouncer, Ricky, who would come over right away. He was a big guy who dressed up like Elvis Presley. The owner finished by telling me I was to start the next day.

I may have made dance-hall history on my first night by being the first person ever to show up for work wearing a long-sleeved, turtleneck sweater. If there was a book entitled *Ripley's Dance Hall Believe It Or Not,* a picture of me in that sweater would be on the cover! When I met the other girls, I was given two pieces of advice on how to attract customers and maximum ticket punch time. The first had to do with my choice of wardrobe selection. As one gum-chewing beauty so succinctly put it: "Ya gotta show 'em your wares, honey." And she was right—on that first night, even though I was asked a few times to dance, there were stretches when I sat completely alone on that long red couch, while a line of men behind the dividing bar just stared at me. Since I was the only person dressed like that in the entire hall, they may have thought I was a waitress who'd sat down to take a break from washing bar glasses. Lesson learned. On my second night, I wore a curve-revealing gown and fared much better.

The second helpful tip was to make the man think, through hints or innuendoes, that there might be a chance he could eventually get a real date with me and see me outside of the confines of the dance hall. I was told that if I did that, it would keep many of the more desperate men coming back to buy my time over and over again. But to me, this second tip having to do with deception was the most wrong. Even the lowest street-corner hooker is straight up honest: "You pay me such and such, and I'll do this and that." End of story.

This brings me to the subject of the men. You would think the only type of person to haunt the dimly lit, smoke-filled halls of the taxi-cab dancing world would be the ones who considered themselves lonely, socially inept losers, pitiful men so lacking in looks, conversational skills and confidence that they knew not what else to do to spend some pleasant, social-time with a woman. I found this somewhat to be true, because there were men who never even asked a girl to dance. Some men would arrive, pay the cover fee, sit down and do nothing for the next few hours but stare at the girls on the couch. How creepy was that?

That notwithstanding, during my short employment, I met a variety of men so different from one another that my curiosity got the best of me. I asked almost every customer that chose me, "Why do you come here?" Three of them stand out in my mind, as clearly as though it was yesterday.

I'll call the first one Arnie.

It was midway through my first night there when Arnie came up and asked me to dance. He was one of those men who considered himself to be a loser on the social scene; a sad, rotund little man in his 30s who still lived with his mother. His hands sweated so profusely that while we danced, I could feel the dampness on my back through my sweater. After a few prim and politely executed turns around the dance floor, we went to a table to sit and talk. I'm a nice person, if I do say so myself, and someone who's easy to talk to—I was genuinely interested in what he had to say.

On my second night there, shortly after my shift started, Arnie showed up again, this time with a bouquet of flowers clutched in his sweaty hand. He came directly up to me as I sat on the red couch, and wiping his other hand on his pants leg, asked me if I wanted to dance. The other girls on the couch, in a professional manner, did not even so much as tilt their heads in our direction, but they saw the eager look on his face as he approached me, flowers in hand—I knew exactly what they were thinking.

I went through the turnstile with him, and then to the bar to get a glass of water to put the flowers in. For a moment, I had roughly the same thought that the couch lizards had: "Locked and loaded on that taxi meter!" But then, my heart sank to my feet. This whole thing was wrong. I had become part of some intricate, desperate fantasy in the eyes of this sad, lonely, little man—the great dance-hall deception! I never meant for that to happen.

We danced one dance then went to a table to talk for a while. I looked at the bouquet of yellow flowers I'd set there before the dance. They were daffodils and very beautiful, but they seemed to glow with pain—his pain.

I said to him, "Arnie, you're a really nice guy. Why do you come here?"

Arnie was silent a few moments, licked his lips, and then slid closer to me on the booth seat. He then slowly and carefully, as though afraid of breaking me, laid his head on my shoulder. There was a complete patheticness to it, if there is such a word.

I sat him up, put my hands on his shoulders, and said, "Arnie, look at me. I like you a lot. I really mean that, but this is not what you think it is, and this is not a good place for you to come." I explained to him why. He got up and left right away, looking very unhappy. I don't know if I helped him or hurt him, but it probably was a combination of the two.

The second man I remember so well I met near the end of my shift on my second night. I'll call him Marty.

Marty was as different from Arnie as two men could possibly be. He was good looking, well dressed, intelligent, confident and urbane, and apparently well-off financially. I wondered what a guy like that was doing in a dimly-lit dive with a dance floor, a bar and a fancy, past-its-prime couch.

We danced then sat at one of the tables to talk for a while. When it was nearing closing time, Marty asked me, in the same relaxed, off-handed, casual way he had been talking about everything else, "If I pay you, will you give me a blow job?" I laughed, and then realized he wasn't joking. I declined, and in the same relaxed, off-handed, casual way, he said, "OK, no problem."

We talked a few more minutes about other things, and then I asked him the golden question: "Why do you come here?" I thought he was going to choke. He looked at me puzzled for a moment, shrugged, looked away indifferently as he regained his composure, and then looked at his watch.

I'd earlier mentioned to him that I had arrived at the hall by bus, and in what I realized now was a carefully-cultivated, social veneer of relaxed casualness, he asked, "How about when this place closes, I take you out to breakfast then I'll give you a ride home?" And he did. He had a beautiful red Ferrari, with all the bells and whistles, in which he drove me to an all-night place for breakfast. He then dropped me off at my house, without so much as a hint of lewdness or an indecent proposal through all of it. We smiled and waved goodbye to each other as he sped off into the night. In hindsight, I'm really glad he wasn't a serial killer.

On my final night, I met the third man, a man I will always remember from those days. I'll call him Henry. He was the only man I encountered who gave me a completely honest answer to my question, "Why do you come here?" And he was the one and only man I met there that I kissed, and I kissed him for real.

Henry was at least 75 years old. It was plain that when he was a young man, he must have been very handsome, because even at his advanced age, there was an aesthetic nobility to his elderly, but unlined, face that you could not help but notice. He was straight and tall, with snow-white hair, clear sky-blue eyes and the kind of bone structure you would see in a classic painting of a god. More than that, though, Henry was a nice man. He was friendly, sincere and clearly content to just be there comfortably engaging in pleasant conversation.

I asked him my question and he answered in an honest, straightforward way. He shared that his wife of many years, whom he had loved deeply, had died a few years earlier and sometimes he felt very lonely. He came to enjoy the company of a pleasant, attractive woman. He didn't want go to some club or bar and have to go through all the social rituals involved with meeting someone and hitting them up or having to cultivate some kind of relationship just to have the company. That's all he really wanted, a few untroubled hours with a nice person, away from his own loneliness. Henry had told me the truth.

I felt sad when he told me this, but glad he chose me as the one to help him wile away the time, because I was exactly what he was looking for that night. And perhaps, when he singled me out on that red couch, in that brief moment of eye contact, he somehow knew I would be the one. I also knew that had I played a musical instrument or poured tea into tiny porcelain cups for him, he would also have enjoyed that just as much.

We spent a great deal of time together that night talking, and once or twice taking to the dance floor. Before he got up to leave, he thanked me with sincerity and kissed me briefly on the mouth. It was sweet, chaste, and it was for real—on my end, too.

I quit working at the dance hall that night. With Henry, I had finally gotten a glimpse into what the world of the successful geisha was really about. And I had my answer as to why men go to places like that—each had his individual story, a hope, a need, or a dream that shimmered like starlight all around that little ticket they punched at the gate.

Mystified by Women

by
Gregory Lamping *

I don't understand women—they mystify me. Just when I think I have them figured out, I find out I haven't. Seems that the one thing I know about them is that I don't know them. I've tried to fathom their minds, but they're always saying and doing things that throw me off guard.

In 1987, a movie came out that was wildly popular with female audiences. Some women saw it over a hundred times, bravely facing a ticket taker who kept grumbling under his breath, "Oh, you again." It had women jumping up out of their seats clapping and cheering and having the time of their lives. The movie was *Dirty Dancing*.

What was it that made women love this movie? I believed that if I could answer that question, I would finally understand them. I wasn't brave enough, however, to buy a theater ticket and risk having that ticket taker say to me, "Whoa, what are you doing here?! *Slumber Party Massacre* is in Theater 3."

Instead, I waited for the movie to be released on video. Once it came out, I rented a copy and pressed PLAY. After rolling my eyes while listening to all this cheesy dialogue ("Nobody puts Baby in a corner.") and speed-searching through these long, drawn-out dance scenes, I got to that moment at the end of the movie when Jennifer Grey runs up to Patrick Swayze on the dance floor and gets held aloft. Ah-ha! So that's it! Women were vicariously reveling in the fantasy of a Plain Jane who transforms herself into a Dancing Queen who then gets swept up into the loving arms of her handsome Prince Charming!

Later that summer, I was working as a nurse at a rehab center when one of the female patients asked me if we had *Dirty Dancing* in our video library. I smiled and told her we did.

"They got it!" she yelled to the other female patients in the dayroom. The male patients, meanwhile, were busy playing cards and didn't bother to look over to see what all the fuss was about.

Those women watched that movie twice that afternoon, laughing, dancing and bopping along to the songs. When that female patient returned the video, I couldn't resist explaining to her my theory on why women were such big fans of that movie. She listened to me with this are-you-done-talking-yet look on her face, before saying, "I just like the dancing."

I had to bite my tongue to keep from saying, "Yeah, right," thinking she was probably too embarrassed to admit she fell for that ugly duckling fairy tale.

Years later I was discussing with my nursing supervisor movies we had liked enough to see more than once. I told her I had seen *Goodfellas* three times, but that it might be bordering on torture for me to see it a fourth time. She told me she had seen *Dirty Dancing* so many times she had lost count. Again, I couldn't resist explaining my theory on why I thought women loved that movie.

"Mmm, I don't know," she said. "I just like the dancing."

To quote Yogi Berra, "It was *déjà vu* all over again." This time, however, I wasn't going to let it go without a fight.

"Come on, now," I said. "Tell me you weren't turned on by Patrick Swayze."

"Actually, he was the one thing in that movie I didn't like. He reminded me too much of those greasers back in high school."

I struggled with what to say next.

"Well, if you like dancing so much, then why don't you do it rather than watch it?"

"My husband hates to dance."

"Oh."

I gave up on arguing with her about what women like. Who am I to say? There are times, however, when women deliberately try to keep us in the dark as to their true nature. For instance, I once overheard a female nurse tell another female nurse this story:

There was a psychiatrist who walked onto the unit limping. The charge nurse noticed his limp and asked him what happened. He told her that he had tripped over his deck, but given his Middle Eastern accent, his pronunciation of "deck" rhymed with "pick" rather than "peck."

"You tripped over . . . what?" she asked.

When he explained that he had tripped over one of the

steps on his "deck," she burst out laughing before telling others about her misunderstanding. That story soon spread like wildfire throughout the hospital.

When the nurse who told the story turned around, I could tell she wasn't expecting to see me sitting there at the nurses' station writing in a patient's chart. She looked horrified.

"Oh, my God!" she said, trembling. "You didn't hear that, did you, Greg?!"

I was surprised she was horrified. Did she really think I would be offended if I heard her say a word that refers to a part of my body I see every morning when I step out of the shower and look in the bathroom mirror?

"Don't worry," I reassured her. "I already heard that story."

I didn't know what to make of her reaction. It's not like I had a reputation around the hospital as a goody two-shoes with a halo above my head.

Several weeks later, something similar happened. One of the nurses I worked with had a joke she wanted to tell everyone—everyone but me. Whenever a female nurse came onto the unit, this nurse would immediately say, "I got this really great joke to tell you, but I can't tell it to you here, not with Greg around. Let's go back to the med room."

She repeated that routine night after night. It got to the point that if I were to hear her say, "NOT WITH GREG AROUND" one more time, I was going to scream and strangle that joke out of her. To keep that from happening, I asked this other nurse, whom I considered a good friend, if she would please tell me the joke.

She was nice enough to tell me. I don't remember anything

about the joke, other than it had to do with a certain sex act practiced by women on women and men on women with a term that rhymes with "Funny King Gus."

What I really wanted to know was why the joke-telling nurse felt the need to exclude me from its telling. So I asked my good friend if she would please explain it to me. From her hems and haws, I could tell this wasn't easy for her.

"Well, you see, uh, when women are with other women and there's no man around, they're different. They're less inhibited and more . . . "

"Raunchy?"

"Well, I wouldn't call it that. Let's just say they're more risqué."

"Why's that?"

"They don't want men to think they're . . . "

"Gross?"

From the look she gave me, I could tell she didn't appreciate my help.

"They're afraid men might see them as less feminine. Telling dirty jokes is supposed to be a guy thing. Women are just as earthy as men, but we don't want them to know that."

Ah ha! So, they're keeping secrets from us men. They want us to make them happy, but they don't want to just come right out and tell us how to do it. They prefer that we learn the hard way, through trial and error.

As a teenager, I thought to please a girl I had to impress her with how impressive I was. ("Look—I can juggle two bottles—oops!") In my early 20s, I read that women liked men who made them laugh, so I pretended to be Bozo the Clown, but I was 99 percent bozo, 1 percent clown. In my 30s, I heard that women wanted men to accept them for who they were and listen to what they had to say. ("Whatever.") In my 40s, I found out women wanted a man who would put down his beer and help with the dishes. ("Hey, I gotta better idea! From now on, why don't we use paper plates and call out for pizza every night?!") When I turned 50, I learned about those four magic words every woman wants to hear from her man: "You are sooooo BEAUTIFUL!"

What I don't understand is why it has to be that word "beautiful." Why can't women settle for "cute" or "pretty" or "attractive?" No, it has to be "beautiful." I know that because I've heard lots of women tell me the same thing, "Either call me beautiful or don't call me at all." If a man shouts from a street corner, "Hey, beautiful!" all the women within earshot will look over, but if he shouts, "Hey, not-so-bad-looking!," forget it.

There are other things I don't understand about women. Such as:

- Why do women always feel that a baby is adorably cute, even if he's got a piggy belly, no teeth, beady eyes and a head that looks like it belongs on some midget truck driver named Otto?
- Why do women consider clothes shopping a recreational activity, but not bass fishing?
- Why do women get mad and take it so personally when you tell them that women take things too personally?
- Why do women always begin their telephone conversations

by asking each other "How are you?" and answering "Fine" before talking about all their problems?

- Why are women scared of mice? Given their size advantage, don't they know they could easily crush them by stomping on them with their feet?
- Why do women feel that it's too dirty a job to take out the trash, but don't mind stuffing the trash bags with dirty diapers?
- Why do women forever feel the need to go out and buy another pair of shoes?

If a woman were to answer all my questions about women, I'd still be going, "Huh? Say that again." The male brain is wired differently from the female brain, and I suspect we have thicker wires, but they're probably not as shiny and pretty.

To my last dying day, I shall continue to be mystified by women, and to that, I say, "Vive la différence!"

Editor's Note: Gregory is our only male author in this anthology. He's a very brave man!

Age is Just a Number

by
Karen Gaebelein

Father Time started creeping up behind me when I reach my mid-30s. I began to see more highlights in my hair, but they weren't added by my hairdresser. And my face was changing; gone was the glow of youth and my once peachy-pink complexion, replaced by a sallow skin tone. I fought these two frightening recognitions with more trips to the hairdresser to camouflage my gray highlights and to the department store to buy jars of goo to help diminish my washed-out skin tone.

Unfortunately, as Father Time marched on, so did my problems. Slowly, things began to change, things that made me realize I truly was getting old. Stepping out of the shower one day resulted in an astonishing revelation—my once perky breasts had become an awning for my feet! And speaking of feet, where did they go? I only see them now when I'm lying down. And talking about lying down, guess where one's sloping chest lands when I lie on my back? My underarms now have their own pillows!

Trips to the department store to expand my wardrobe revealed a clothing conspiracy against very ample sized, 40-plus-year-old women. During one recent trip, I received a warm greeting from the salesclerk. She looked all of 12 years old and weighed all of 6 pounds. She asked if she could help me with my clothing selection.

"Who keeps putting size-14 tags on size-8 clothes?" was my first question. Miss Six Pounds responded that perhaps the clothes did not fit because of the cut or style. *Who cut them? Barbie? I* thought. *Barbie and a number-two pencil are the only two things I know of that have a waist that small.*

Miss Six Pounds graciously escorted me to the plus-size department and selected several outfits for me that were big enough to cover a car. "Thank you, no!" I said. "I'm not a size 8, but I'm also not an Oldsmobile."

Reminders of my middle-aged blues journey also surfaced when I made my yearly jaunt to the gynecologist. My last trip made me feel very ancient as I was greeted by yet another 12-year-old who updated my file. Miss Twelve-Year-Old then escorted me to the examination room. I donned my paper gown and waited for my doctor.

"How are you, Karen?" the doctor asked as he entered the room. "Having any problems?"

"Well, my monthly cycle is now semi-monthly, my PMS is worse and my body temperature always seems to be at least 101 degrees."

He looked at my records. "Karen, you're 48 now. You do realize you've reached a time in your life where your body will be going through changes, right?"

"Yes, but when will these changes stop?"

"Never," the doctor responded. "You will just have to get used to them."

"Isn't there a pill or vitamin or herb or something I can take to feel better?"

"No, not really," this wise and knowing man replied. "Vitamins and herbs won't hurt you, but we really haven't come up with a good solution for helping women at this particular crossroads in their lives."

I thought to myself, *Those are dressed-up words for, "You're old, sweetheart—deal with it!"* Why did I suddenly feel like Helen Hayes? *Crossroads? What crossroads?* As the doctor left and I trashed their designer paper gown, smiling Miss Twelve-Year-Old reappeared with a prescription and free samples of Geritol and Metamucil.

"Here you are, ma'am. Maybe these will make you feel better. Would you like me to stick these samples in your bag?"

Resisting the urge to tell her where to stick them, I bit my tongue, flashed my show-biz smile and responded with the affirmative.

As I left the doctor's office, I stopped at the cafe in his building to ponder my fate. I purchased a Diet Pepsi and discarded the Geritol and Metamucil. Making my way to a table, I quickly glanced at the other customers in the cafe. No 12-year-olds! No Barbies! Just regular folks sitting down eating and drinking. What fun!

These other customers provided me with a reprieve from feeling like a worn-out piece of elastic. I started to think about the good, the bad and the ugly times of my life. Do I really want to be 12 years old again? *I don't think so!* Do I really want to look like a number-two pencil? *No, that might make it hard to figure out which way to put on my clothes.* Is age really relevant? *No, it's the attitude that's important. Father Time will keep on marching regardless of how much I whine.*

Right then and there, I decided to buy one of those 18-hour Playtex something-or-others to hoist up those parts of me sloping toward my feet, put it on with gusto and march right along with Father Time. After all, I've learned that age is just a number!

A Chocolate Coffee Paradox

by
Diana M. Amadeo

Contentment, peace and happiness can be found in the most ordinary places. I never thought I'd have such profound thoughts while killing time with coffee and samples of chocolate. Yet here I was once again contemplating life's events and solving world problems.

There is a shop close to my home where chocolatiers make premium candy in front of their customers. It's a smaller version of Willie Wonka's chocolate factory, and yet, to my knowledge, no visiting children have been lost in its machinery. There is no ingenious and insane man in a purple hat standing back to admire his creation, and no little men in white suits scurrying around performing mundane tasks. Likewise, there fails to be a ribbon of thick brown liquid being churned out of a melting pot and flowing like a river to parts unknown.

Still, the store smells like I imagine heaven should. The female proprietor has wisely placed large windows so you can watch the pure chocolate being poured and molded into individual candy portions. Inside, a small tray of samples is available where you can indulge as you watch. Sometimes the chocolate fountain is running, and you can dip strawberries into the sweet brown confection.

The store area is tiny, with no restaurant facility, but there is always a pot of coffee brewing. And they offer my favorite flavor of coffee—Dark Sin. I'd like to think that this exquisite blend of hazelnut-, cinnamon- and chocolate-flavored coffee is designed, blended, roasted and perked just for me. (But I do let other customers purchase it, too.)

Ordinarily, as a chocoholic, I would avoid going into a shop that carried the source of my addiction. I patronize the shop just for the coffee . . . and maybe a sample or two of chocolate. Free candy is like a broken cookie—it has no calories and therefore, supports no addiction or guilt. It seems this paradox is part of the some divine plan, a quasi mini-heaven on earth. Since this entire scenario seems to be ordained by some higher being, it would be scandalous of me not to imbibe in such confectionary devilish delight.

Sipping on some Dark Sin and thoughtfully nibbling on some free chocolates may seem a colossal waste of time to most people. But I don't see it that way. In my idleness, as warm coffee soothes the throat and the milk chocolate teases my taste buds, many of life's problems and complexities are solved in my mind.

I feel a spiritual connection to Forrest Gump's mother, who sees life "like a box of chocolates, you just never know what you're going to get." Some prefer pure dark chocolate, others require a little filling, and still others prefer nuts with just a smattering of chocolate. That's OK. I don't force my opinion or particular taste onto anyone. And I'd prefer they not force their beliefs onto me. Variety is the spice of life. Different beliefs, faiths, customs and ceremony have made this country great. I can't imagine living in a society where one particular type of chocolate was forced down the throat of anyone. Or, God forbid, we were all forced to drink plain, black, unflavored coffee.

Over the years I have watched the contrariness of life. Sometimes I voice protest, most often, I watch at a distance. Coffee and chocolate have made me more contemplative, more thoughtful with how the world turns. As I bite into a caramel-filled, white-chocolate truffle, it occurs to me that anything, anyone or any concept can be distorted, manipulated, spun and lied about to fit any context desired. But like Forrest Gump, I scratch my head and wonder why life's squares are forced into round pegs. A sigh and a sip of Dark Sin accompany the hope for truth and justice. Another sip admits that truth and justice are often denied.

While savoring a dark chocolate-covered cherry, I wonder about good versus bad and the paradoxes of life. Why do Americans get fatter as the diet industry balloons? Most religions preach love, hope and joy, yet the world is constantly at hateful war. Alternative fuel sources are many to be had, yet we pollute and pillage the earth over fossil fuels. And we know to conserve our limited gas supply, yet we purchase oversized pick-up trucks and SUVs.

A tiny piece of almond bark transports me into another

line of thought and confronts further dilemma. Peace can be found through silence and introspection, but we mask silence with iPods, televisions and cell phones. Beauty and health can be found in the breeze and sunshine outdoors, yet we lose our vitamin and energy stores under banks of fluorescent lights and stale ventilation.

A bite of cream-filled chocolate precedes the thought that we indeed live in confusing, intolerant and paradoxical times. Depression, stress, anxiety and insomnia seem the norm. As life gets more and more complex, we search for simple, honest answers. I've given this a lot of thought, and this is what I have found: Take it easy. Be idle. Sit back and watch the world. Things grow and change. Life's not an everlasting gobstopper that never gets smaller. There is no Willy Wonka chewing gum that never loses its flavor, size or constancy. This is pure fantasy. To live is to evolve, to be flexible and accept that which supports life.

But then again, maybe some of the best answers to life's greatest questions can be found with fine chocolate samples melting in your mouth while you're sipping some Dark Sin.

A Catholic Schoolgirl's Primer

by
Carole Ann Moleti

The first time I ever saw a condom was in the late 1960s, when I was about 8 years old. It floated like a translucent, bloated hot dog in the water under the dock near my backyard.

"Don't jump on the jellyfish!" I yelled to my friend.

"That's not a jellyfish. It's a poison sock." Ann spoke with the authority of an 11-year-old.

"Where do they come from?"

"From fish shedding their skin. My mother said to never touch them."

Ann was always right. We waited until the tide carried the poison sock away and enjoyed the rest of the day splashing in the water, never stopping to think what else might be lurking out there.

I once saw one when fishing with my father. "Look, a poison sock. Ann says they come from fish shedding their skin."

I don't recall Daddy's response. He probably just said the same thing he did when I made the astute observation that his male pigeons always climbed on top of the females when they were playing. "How do you like that?"

I was 10 the first time I heard anything about puberty and sex. Beads of sweat glistened on Mommy's brow and she couldn't look me in the eye. She summoned the courage to interrupt me, while I was watching *Lost in Space*, to hand over a Kotex kit containing sanitary napkins, pins, belts and two booklets.

Within the pages of the pink book were a drawing of the female reproductive system and all sorts of useful tips about menstrual periods, such as why you got them, how to use sanitary napkins and where to dispose of them—but to never flush them down the toilet. This new information was never going to convince me to turn off the television.

The blue book had a drawing of the male reproductive system and some sperm-meets-egg allusions. Something like when a man and woman are in love they hold each other very close, magic happens, and nine months later a stork delivers the baby. Much more interesting.

I finished watching *Lost in Space*, pondering how Judy handled her periods since she had been lost in space for years. I wondered if Don knew when she had her period. He was the first mate, but destined to become her husband, because, after all, they were lost in space and there was little hope they'd ever find their way back to Earth. Proper disposal of whatever sanitary napkins she had, while confined on a tiny spaceship, had to be an issue.

I wondered if men were supposed to know when women

had their periods or if it was just this secret females shared only among themselves. I placed my Kotex kit proudly on the desk in my room for all to see. When I went back upstairs, my mother had hidden it in the closet and the blue book had disappeared. I decided right then this was not going to be a fun experience.

Sometime during eighth grade, the class was separated. The boys went with Monsignor Devlin, who was old, Irish, and threatened everyone with the Fires of Hell for any infraction of the rules. The girls went with Sister Jean Marie. She was young, Irish, and threatened everyone with the Fires of Hell for infractions of rules like eating meat on Friday.

Each assemblage endured the "talk." I don't remember too much about what Sister shared with our group, but since we all had gotten our first periods by then, she was a year too late. We already knew how to use the belts and safety pins in an emergency, and how to dispose of Kotex properly—never flushing them, of course.

I remember my father being very upset about this and yelling at my mother while she ironed that night. Mommy didn't say anything. He called me into the room and demanded I tell him exactly what Sister had said.

"She talked about men-stru-a-tion and that stuff," I responded. Sister had made a point of diagramming the word so we would know the proper way to pronounce it.

I felt the flush rise on my cheeks and my heart pound, hoping Daddy knew what periods were because I really didn't want to get into the details of how it felt to walk around wearing a wad of paper saturated with blood between my legs, held in place by a slippery elastic belt or a safety pin. It made hopscotch really hard and jumping Double Dutch impossible.

"That's all they told you?"

"Yes, that's all." I escaped before he could ask anything else.

The next day, Kenny, who had a crush on me, asked why Monsignor told the boys they should never look inside a girl's purse. "What do you keep in there that we should never see?"

"I have no idea what you're talking about," I lied. This was a secret for just us girls.

It wasn't until my boyfriend Michael, who was three years older than me, made a comment that I must be on the rag since I was so bitchy that I found out that they do get some information.

"You try walking around with a wad of paper saturated with blood between your legs for five days, every month, and see how happy you feel," I told him.

The first time I ever used a tampon was on the Labor Day I turned 14. I'd trained all summer to compete in a swimming race that holiday weekend, but my period arrived a few days early. I had no idea what excuse to give my father for bowing out. Fighting back tears, I asked my mother, who dutifully bought me the Kotex super-16 pack every month and a girdle, instead of those stupid belts and safety pins.

"You can still swim. Use these." She handed me a box much smaller than the one I'd learned to despise. "Read the directions. Go into the bathroom. You'll figure it out."

Finally, an accurate anatomy chart showing all three holes! I saved it to show my friends. That and the part that says you do not lose your virginity if you use tampons. It took me about two hours and almost the entire box before I mastered the new devices. I've been a torchbearer for Tampax ever since. They can be flushed!

Having conquered the material in the pink book, I got to work on the blue one. The first time I did more than peck my boyfriend on the cheek, I panicked.

"You can't get pregnant like that," Linda tried to convince me during a rehearsal break for the musical *Dames at Sea*.

My character was Trixie; she was Bubbles. I didn't believe her and kept crying, convinced that I was pregnant since Michael, who was playing one of the sailors, had held me really close backstage, kissed me, touched my behind and between my thighs.

Michael later told me to stop being stupid—the only way for me to get pregnant was if we were undressed and he put his penis inside my vagina. "We didn't do that, and if we do, I have to use a condom so you won't get pregnant."

That wasn't written in any of the books. "How do you know that?"

"My friends told me."

"What's a condom?" I asked.

Carole Ann

NYMB Creators

Together, Dahlynn and Ken McKowen have 60-plus years of professional writing, editing, publication, marketing and public relations experience. Full-time authors and travel writers, the two have such a large body of freelance work that when they reached more than 2,000 articles, stories and photographs published, they stopped counting. And the McKowens are well respected ghostwriters, having worked with CEOs and founders of some of the nation's biggest companies. They have even ghostwritten for a former U.S. president and a few California governors and elected officials.

From 1999 to 2009, Ken and Dahlynn were consultants and coauthors for *Chicken Soup for the Soul*, where they collaborated with series founders Jack Canfield and Mark Victor Hansen on several books such as *Chicken Soup for the Entrepreneur's Soul; Chicken Soup for the Soul in Menopause; Chicken Soup for the Fisherman's Soul;* and *Chicken Soup for the Soul: Celebrating Brothers and Sisters.* They also edited and ghost-created many more Chicken titles during their tenure, with Dahlynn reading more than 100,000 story submissions.

For highly acclaimed outdoor publisher Wilderness Press, the McKowen's books included national award-winner *Best of California's Missions, Mansions and Museums; Best of Oregon and Washington's Mansions, Museums and More;* and *The Wine-Oh! Guide to California's Sierra Foothills.*

Under Publishing Syndicate, the couple authored and published *Wine Wherever: In California's Mid-Coast & Inland Region*, and are actively researching wineries for *Wine Wherever: In California's Paso Robles Region*, the second book in the Wine Wherever series.

If that's not enough, the McKowens are also the creators of the Wine Wherever iPhone mobile winery-destination journaling app and are currently creating a travel television show under the same brand (www.WineWherever.com).

Dahlynn and Ken in their backyard.

Contributor Bios

Kendra Alvey lives in Los Angeles with her husband, Tim, and her dog, Hogan McSmalls. Her essay "Being Elmo" was published in the anthology *HerStory: What I Learned in My Bathtub.* You can also find her work online at TheImpersonals.com or her own blog: www. Kendragarden.com. She is @Kendragarden on Twitter.

Diana M. Amadeo is a multi award-winning author and has published hundreds of works in books, e-books, magazines, newspapers and online. She resides with her family in a woodsy retreat in New England.

Kathleene Baker resides in Plano, Texas with husband Jerry and three furry kids: Hank, Samantha and Abby. She has contributed to many publications, online newsletters, newspapers, *Chicken Soup for the Soul* and writes weekly, monthly and quarterly columns/articles. Kathy regularly promotes animal rescue groups and is especially passionate about dogs.

Valerie Benko is a communications specialist from western Pennsylvania. She received her bachelor's degree from Slippery Rock University in 2002, where she majored in journalism and creative writing. Her creative nonfiction has appeared in several anthology series including *Chicken Soup for the Soul.* Visit her online at http:// valeriebenko@weebly.com.

Mary A. Berger is a humor-mystery novelist of the *Mattie Mitchell Mystery* series. Her writing has appeared in *The Saturday Evening Post, Lady's Circle,* various small press and writer's publications. But with all that, she says she still finds time to "get muddy!" Visit her at mattiesmysteries.blogspot.com.

Sylvia Bright-Green, in her 35-year writing career, has been published in 12 anthologies and coauthored two books. She has published hundreds of manuscripts to newspapers to magazines. She is actively involved in her local and state writers' clubs, and in the oldest spiritual/metaphysical group in Wisconsin.

Debra Ayers Brown is a writer, humorist, blogger, magazine columnist and award-winning marketing professional. Her stories have been in *Guideposts, Liberty Life, Chicken Soup for the Soul* and others. Debra is involved in Southeastern Writers Association, Humor Writers of America, Southern Humorists, Georgia Writers Association and She Writes. See her websites www.About.Me/DebraAyersBrown and www.DebraAyersBrown.com

Sallie Wagner Brown used to be a race car driver and a teacher; now she is a boater, a traveler and a writer. She, her husband and three dogs live on Hood Canal in northwest Washington state where her surroundings both inspire her and make it difficult to concentrate.

Marcia Byalick is a young adult novelist, columnist for several Long Island publications, frequent contributor to the *New York Times* and *Newsday*, and a teacher of memoir writing. She loves sharing the stories of her life and hopes to encourage others to write their stories before their words are lost forever.

Kathe Campbell lives her dream on a Montana mountain with her mammoth donkeys, a Keeshond and kitties. Three children, 11 grandkids and four greats round out the herd. She is a prolific writer on Alzheimer's and is a contributing author to the *Chicken Soup for the Soul* series, medical journals and magazines.

Barbara Carpenter is an avid reader who has read thousands of books. Her works include a three-book series, *Starlight, Starbright . . .* , two memoirs, multiple stories for *Chicken Soup* books, as well as award-winning short stories and poetry. Four novels are in progress. Her family includes a husband, two children, five grandchildren and a dog.

Elynne Chaplik-Aleskow is a Pushcart Prize nominated author and award-winning educator and broadcaster. She is founding general manager of WYCC-TV/PBS and distinguished professor emeritus of Wright College in Chicago. Her stories and essays have been published in numerous anthologies and magazines. Visit http://LookAroundMe.blogspot.com.

Ellen Denton is a freelance writer living in the Rocky Mountains with her husband and two demonic cats who wreak havoc on a regular basis (the cats, not the husband).

Terri Duncan, a high school administrator, is a devoted wife and mother of two grown children. She hopes they support her in her retirement so she can pursue her dream of writing. Terri has authored numerous short stories and a book for young readers—*Camping Reservations: Body of Lies.*

Terri Elders, LCSW, lives with two dogs and three cats near Colville, Washington. Her stories have appeared in dozens of periodicals and anthologies. She blogs at www.atouchoftarragon.blogspot.com.

Laura Farkas lives in Michigan where she is raising her children and continuing the foundation of her late husband's fishing lure company. She enjoys chocolate, the outdoors and writing for *Frank Talk* entertainment magazine.

Sara Foore currently lives in Buffalo, New York, as a single thirty-something. This is her first venture into sharing her work in a public forum. When she isn't dating, she enjoys spending time with family, friends and her adorable Greyhound. She wants to thank her family for their unwavering support.

Karen Gaebelein enjoys writing about everyday topics, using her great sense of humor to engage her readers and make them laugh. Her stories have been published in many forums, including the popular *Chicken Soup for the Soul* series. You can reach Karen at gabe501@aol.com.

Monica Giglio (www.monicagiglio.com) is an artist and writer whose works have been published in *Welcome Home Magazine* and *Chicken Soup for the Soul*. Her column "Monica's Corner" appears in *Showcase Magazine*. The Arts in Embassies program currently exhibits her art in Tashkent, Uzbekistan, at the ambassadorial residence. Monicagiglio@optonline.net

T'Mara Goodsell is a multi-genre writer, teacher and single mother who lives near St. Louis, Missouri. She has written for *Chicken Soup for the Soul* as well as other anthologies, newspapers and publications.

Dianna Graveman is a former corporate training designer, elementary- and middle-school teacher, book and magazine editor, and MFA faculty member. She currently teaches writing workshops and freelances as a writer, editor and designer through her company, 2 Rivers Communications & Design, LLC. Read more at www.2riverscommunications.com and www.DiannaGraveman.com.

Stacey Gustafson received her bachelor of arts from Washington University in St. Louis. She writes humorous short stories based on her suburban family and everyday life. Most readers relate to her experiences and enjoy the laughable perspective. She lives in Pleasanton, California with her husband and two children. Email: gustafson1@comcast.net

Marijo Herndon has written for *Chicken Soup for the Soul* books, *Simple Joy, Nights and Weekends, The Daily Gazette* and the book, *One Touch from the Maker*. She lives in New York with her husband Dave, and two cats—Lucy and Ethel.

Erika Hoffman is a former teacher, a mom, a daughter, a friend to many and a wannabe Erma Bombeck.

Mary Horner is the author of *Strengthen Your Nonfiction Writing*. She teaches communications at St. Louis Community College and blogs about writing at writRteachR.blogspot.com.

Georgia A. Hubley retired after 20 years from financial management to write fulltime. Vignettes of her life have been published in *Woman's World, Chicken Soup for the Soul* book series, *Hallmark* book series, other anthologies and periodicals. Two grown sons have left the nest, and she resides with her husband in Henderson, Nevada.

Caroleah Johnson is a wife, mom, grandma, retired dental hygienist, health coach, personal chef and writer. She lives in the mountains of Northern California where she spends a good amount of time cleaning up pine needles. She still cannot back up a trailer, though.

Mary-Lane Kamberg gets her hair done once a month whether she needs it or not. She has published 22 books, including the *I Don't Know How to Cook* book (Adams Media) and the *I Love to Write Book* (Crickhollow Books). She is co-leader of the Kansas City Writers Group.

Janet Sheppard Kelleher is a Southern columnist who enjoys hunting, fishing and zip-lining. Oh, my! She earned a Sweet Briar College mathematics degree and wrote a humorous gift book about coping with breast cancer—*BIG C, Little Ta-Ta*—which won the Southeastern Writers' Association's Hal Bernard Award for nonfiction. It debuts in 2013.

Ginger Kenchel is a comic at heart. When asked how she stays looking so young, she replies, "Lady Clairol and Oil of Olay, they make me the woman I am today."

Cathi LaMarche resides with her husband, two children and three spoiled dogs in Missouri. She has numerous essays published in various anthologies and is the author of the novel *While the Daffodils Danced*. Cathi has a master's degree and teaches composition and literature. She is working on her second novel.

Gregory Lamping is a psychiatric nurse living in Kirkwood, Missouri. He's still mystified by women, but since he's been working alongside them most of his life, he's getting to know them a little better.

Lisa McManus Lange lives in Victoria, BC, Canada. When not chasing boys—her own sons, that is—she is a multi-published writer of humorous and inspirational slice-of-life articles. Write her at lisamc2010@yahoo.ca or visit her at www.lisamcmanuslange.blogspot.com.

Sandie Lee has been writing for 18 years. She has been published online and in print in both children's and women's genres. She currently lives in Ontario, Canada, with her hubby of 15 years and two feline "children."

Ruth Littner is a partner in Gemini Wordsmiths, an editing and copywriting company. Ruth penned *Living with Ghosts*, a nonfiction narrative detailing the ripple effects of the horrors of the Holocaust on three generations, and the unintentional transference of PTSD from her Holocaust-surviving parents to Ruth and to her children.

Glady Martin lives in a small hamlet in British Columbia, Canada where she enjoys sharing her stories through words. Having written since grade school, she says, "Writing is a way of breathing for me . . . it is a wonderful tool for expressing myself." Glady also enjoys writing poetry.

Laurel (Bernier) McHargue was raised as "Daughter #4" of five girls in Braintree, Massachusetts, where she lived until heading off to Smith College, followed by the United States Military Academy. Her constant quest for adventure landed her in Leadville, Colorado, where she currently resides with her husband and two sons.

Carole Ann Moleti works as a nurse-midwife in New York City. Her fiction and nonfiction focuses on women's and political issues. This essay is from her memoir *Someday I'm Going to Write a Book: Diary of an Urban Missionary*. She is at work on a mommy memoir *Karma, Kickbacks and Kids.*

Alice Muschany lives in Flint Hill, Missouri. Recently retired, her hobbies include hiking, swimming, photography and writing. Alice's eight grandchildren make wonderful subjects.

Pat Nelson is a contributor to *Not Your Mother's Book...On Being a Stupid Kid* and *On Dogs*. She is co-creator on *Not Your Mother's Book...On Parenting*, *On Grandparenting* and *On Working for a Living*. She has written newspaper columns, contributed to *Chicken Soup for the Soul* and written one book, *You . . . The Credit Union Member.*

Wendy Nelson lives by the beautiful shores of Lake Simcoe, Ontario, Canada, with her amazing husband and two young sons. When she's not busy being a hockey mom, you can find her with notebook in hand, and two dogs in tow, writing short stories and dark thrillers.

Susan Nickerson's short stories have appeared in several publications including *Palm Prints Literary Journal*, *Compassionate Friends Magazine* and *Open Minds Quarterly*. Chapter One of Susan's novel, *Amazing Grace*, recently placed third in the 2012 Writers-Editors International Writing Competition. She lives in Florida with her husband Peter and their dog Riley.

Linda O'Connell, a preschool teacher from St. Louis, Missouri, is an award-winning inspirational and humor writer. Her husband, children and grandchildren fill her life with happiness and her heart with love. Linda blogs at www.http//lindaoconnell.blogspot.com.

Elsilee Patterson received her degree and lifetime teaching credential from San Diego State University. She pursued her beloved calling, teaching children for 35 years, retiring in 2003. While continuing her formal education, she also finds life a most amazing classroom and every person an unpredictable, though fascinating, teacher.

Rose Ella Putnam is 92 years old. After raising three children and outliving her husband of 59-1/2 years, Rose Ella has many nonfiction stories to tell. She enjoys playing cribbage at the senior center and sharing stories of her life at the Write Your Life Story group in Longview, Washington.

Cappy Hall Rearick is a syndicated newspaper columnist, award-winning short story writer and author of six published books and five successful columns. Featured by the Erma Bombeck Writers Workshop as a Humor Writer of the Month, Rearick's humor and short fiction has been read and enjoyed in anthologies throughout the country.

Sallie Rodman received her professional writing credential from California State University, Long Beach in 1996. She has been contributing to *Chicken Soup for the Soul,* various other anthologies and magazines ever since. She loves to write about real-life events. Catch her at sa.rodman@verizon.net.

Sioux Roslawski's musings can be found at SiouxsPage.blogspot. com. She is a third grade teacher, a dog rescuer, a freelance writer and a consultant for the Gateway Writing Project, part of the National Writing Project Network. Daily she reads, she writes and she battles hot flashes!

Joyce Newman Scott worked as a flight attendant while pursuing an acting career. She started college in her mid-50s and studied at the University of Miami and at Florida International University. She is currently working on a memoir, a television script and a feature film. Please contact her at jnewmansco@aol.com.

Elizabeth Bussey Sowdal is a registered nurse and freelance writer who lives and works in Oklahoma. She is a recent grandmother who advocates the consumption of sweets, the shedding of shoes, the flouting of rules and all manner of other poor behavior.

Terri Spilman is a writer living by the mantra "at least it will make a good story." Several of her stories have received recognition by *Humor Press* and she has been featured on *Freshly Pressed* on Wordpress.com. She specializes in humor essays and commentary in her blog, thelaughingmom.wordpress.com.

Pam Suwinsky lives in Sacramento, California. She is the author of a book-in-progress: *Bloomers: Adventures in Lingerie Management: True-Life Stories of Wardrobe Malfunctions and How We Survived Them.*

Janet Hall Svisdahl has been a frequent contributor to the *Chicken Soup for the Soul* series and has recently published her first cookbook entitled *Cooking with Spirits for the Spirit*, due to be out on book shelves Christmas 2012. She has also written and published several short fantasies.

Donna Collins Tinsley—wife, mother and grandmother—lives in Port Orange, Florida. Her work has been published in several magazines and book compilations. Find her on Facebook, at thornrose7. blogspot.com, or email her at Thornrose7@aol.com.

Tina Traster is a *New York Post* columnist, a *Huffington Post* blogger and an essayist. Her work has appeared in newspapers, magazines, literary journals and on NPR. She's been anthologized in literary collections *Living Lessons* and *Mammas and Pappas*. Traster is writing a memoir about her adopted Russian daughter.

Mary Eileen Williams is the founder/host of the popular blog and radio show *Feisty Side of Fifty* (www.feistysideoffifty.com). A long-time career coach with a master's degree in career development, she is the author of the book *Land the Job You Love* and writes a job search column for the *Huffington Post.*

Nancy Withers is now retired after teaching for 40 years. She enjoys writing stories for children, especially her five granddaughters. She also loves a good puzzle, crossword, Sudoku, cryptograph, jumble, even jigsaw. Nancy is the author of the upcoming children's picture book *The Creaky House*, due out in 2014.

Story Permissions

A Chocolate Coffee Paradox © 2010 Diana M. Amadeo
Sarong, So Right © 2012 Debra Brown
Three and I'm Out © 2012 Kathleene S. Baker
Almost Barely Complete © 2012 Valerie Benko
Die-Hard Eager Beaver © 2001 Mary A. Berger
Your Hard Drive's Corrupted © 2011 Sylvia Bright-Green
The Force of Eds © 2012 Sallie Lyla Brown
Not-So-Sweet Revenge © 2010 Marcia Byalick
No Mountain Too High © 2006 Kathleen M. Campbell
Smack Down © 2012 Barbara Carpenter
The Revolving Door © 2006 Elynne Chaplik-Aleskow
Dance Hall Girl © 2012 Ellen Denton
The Princess and the Pimp © 2011 Ellen Denton
Dressing to Kill is Killing Me © 2012 Terri Duncan
Egged On © 2010 Theresa J. Elders
Up Front © 2008 Theresa J. Elders
Tawdry Behavior © 2010 Laura Farkas
Single and Searching © 2012 Sara Foore
Age is Just a Number © 2012 Karen Gaebelein
The Ice Bra Cometh © 2012 Monica Giglio
Worse Than Zombie Warts © 2012 T'Mara Goodsell
Cream or Sugar? © 2012 Dianna Graveman
Hair Gone Wild © 2012 Patch Inc. Used with permission.
Peace in Pandemonium © 2007 Marijo Herndon
Starve Yourself Thin © 2012 Marijo Herndon
Booby Trapped © 2010 Erika Hoffman
Size 14 is Not a Curse © 2007 Mary Horner
Only a Coincidence © 2012 Georgia A. Hubley
Backing Up © 2012 Caroleah Johnson
Zigzagging © 2012 Caroleah Johnson
It's Gotta be the Hair © 2003 Mary-Lane Kamberg
Sitting Room Only © 2012 Janet Sheppard Kelleher
For Better or For Worse © 2006 Virginia Kenchel
Come Rain or Shine © 2012 Cathi LaMarche
Mystified by Women © 2012 Gregory Lamping
No More Should © 2012 Lisa Lange
The Windy Dress © 2011 Glady Martin
Battle-Dressed Breasts © 2012 Laurel J. McHargue
A Catholic Schoolgirl's Primer © 2007 Carole Ann Moleti

Spam-in-a-Can © 2011 Sandra Lee Muncaster
Will He Notice Me Then? © 2011 Sandra Lee Muncaster
High Five © 2012 Alice E. Muschany
Blind-Sighted © 2007 Patricia A. Nelson
The Must-Have © 2012 Wendy Nelson
Tan Lines © 2007 Susan J. Nickerson
Suck it Up © 2012 Linda O'Connell
Everything's Bigger in Texas © 2008 Kendra Alvey Parsons
Life's a Classroom © 2012 Elsie Lee Patterson
And Me Without a Crotch © 2012 Rose Ella Putnam
It's a Wrap © 2011 Cappy Hall Rearick
Give a Woman a Gun © 2012 Sallie A. Rodman
To the Brink and Back © 2012 Sioux Roslawski
The Pinup Girl © 2004 Joyce Newman Scott
The Price is Right © 2011 Ruth Littner Shaw
Granny Pants © 2008 Elizabeth Nadine Sowdal
Honey, You're a Fat Ass © 2012 Terri L. Spilman
Vajazzle My What? © 2011 Terri L. Spilman
W—The Other Scarlet Letter © 2012 Terri L. Spilman
Dinner Dance Drama © 2010 Pam Suwinsky
Harley and the Harridan © 2004 Janet Svisdahl
Got Love Handles? © 2012 Donna Collins Tinsley
For Your Convenience © 2010 Tina Traster
Stirred, Not Shaken © 2006 Mary Eileen Williams
It All Depends © 2012 Nancy Jean Withers

Photo Credits

Page 5   Photo by Claire Freise
Page 19   Photo by Darryl Nelson
Page 59   Photo by Julie Smith
Page 69   Photo by Susan Nickerson
Page 88   Photo by Gertie Simmons
Page 92   Photo by Charles Bernier
Page 105 Photo by Alex Marie LaSalla
Page 113 Photo by Wiley Svisdahl
Page 205 Photo by Jeffrey Grant
Page 283 Photo by Shawn Shiflet

Publishing Syndicate

Publishing Syndicate LLC is an independent book publisher based in Northern California. The company has been in business for more than a decade, mainly providing writing, ghostwriting and editing services for major publishers. In 2011, Publishing Syndicate took the next step and expanded into a full-service publishing house.

The company is owned by married couple Dahlynn and Ken McKowen. Dahlynn is the CEO and publisher, and Ken serves as president and managing editor.

Publishing Syndicate's mission is to help writers and authors realize personal success in the publishing industry, and, at the same time, provide an entertaining reading experience for its customers. From hands-on book consultation and their very popular and free monthly *Wow Principles* publishing tips e-newsletter to forging book deals with both new and experienced authors and launching three new anthology series, Publishing Syndicate has created a powerful and enriching environment for those who want to share their writing with the world. (www.PublishingSyndicate.com)

NYMB Needs Your Stories!

We are looking for hip, fun, modern and very-much-today type stories, just like those in this book, for 30 new titles in the *NYMB* series. Published contributors are compensated.

Submission guidelines at www.PublishingSyndicate.com

More *NYMB* Titles

Look for new
Not Your Mother's Books
coming soon!

**_Do you know a teen with
a great story to share?_**

OMG! My Reality!
For Teens

Publishing Syndicate is now accepting stories for our new teen anthology series!

This new anthology will feature a collection of personal real-life stories written by and about teens. We are looking for humorous, heart-warming and inspiring stories **written by individuals 25 years old and younger about teen life.**

If you have a story to share about a personal experience that will touch the hearts, lives and souls of teens, we would love to consider it for publication in *OMG! My Reality! For Teens*. Royalties will be paid to those whose stories make the final cut.

For more information and to read submission guidelines, please visit the website below. And tell your friends, too!

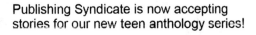